FIGHTING FIRE!

FIGHTING FIRE!

Ten of the Deadliest Fires in American History and How We Fought Them

MICHAEL L. COOPER

Henry Holt and Company ✷ New York

Henry Holt and Company, LLC
Publishers since 1866
175 Fifth Avenue
New York, New York 10010
mackids.com

Library of Congress Cataloging-in-Publication Data is available.

ISBN 978-0-8050-9714-6

Henry Holt books may be purchased for business or promotional use. For information on bulk purchases, please contact Macmillan Corporate and Premium Sales Department at (800) 221-7945 x5442 or by e-mail at specialmarkets@macmillan.com.

First Edition—2014 / Designed by Meredith Pratt
Printed in the United States of America by R. R. Donnelley & Sons Company,
Harrisonburg, Virginia

1 3 5 7 9 10 8 6 4 2

To my New York friends Russell and Jim
who have always been so supportive

CONTENTS

THE AMERICAN FIREMAN.

FIGHTING FIRE!

INTRODUCTION

A "dreadful city of fire" is how one visitor described colonial Boston. That's because fires frequently destroyed large sections of the city.

But it wasn't a problem only in Boston or in the colonial era. Major fires regularly leveled cities up until the early twentieth century.

Several of these fires shaped history. King George's indifference to the suffering of Boston's citizens after the big fire of 1760, some historians believe, added to the tensions that sparked the American Revolution. New York City's Great Fire of 1835 prompted the building of the Croton Aqueduct, one of the nineteenth century's grandest engineering feats. And the Great

Chicago Fire of 1871 cleared the way for a new style of architecture that reshaped skylines around the world—the skyscraper.

Many smaller American fires were no less significant in terms of developing firefighting and fire-safety techniques. In the early twentieth century, a fire aboard the *General Slocum,* a popular excursion boat in New York City, killed 1,021 people. A few months later in the same city, the Triangle Shirtwaist Company fire killed 146 young garment workers. Big or small, each fire resulted in innovations as well as stronger laws and regulations. Science and technology improved fire protection, fire detection, and firefighting.

Despite these advances, fire is still a major threat. According to the National Fire Protection Association, U.S. fire departments responded to nearly 1.3 million fires in 2010. That's one every 24 seconds. Those fires caused $11.6 billion in damage and killed 3,125 people, not including firefighters.

Even with today's technology, tragedies still occur. In late June 2013, a wildfire in central Arizona trapped and killed an elite group of 19 firefighters. Two months later, the Rim Fire, one of California's biggest wildfires, burned more than 370 square miles of land, including a large portion of Yosemite National Park. It

SEATTL
in 188

SAN FRANCISC
in 1851 and
again in 190

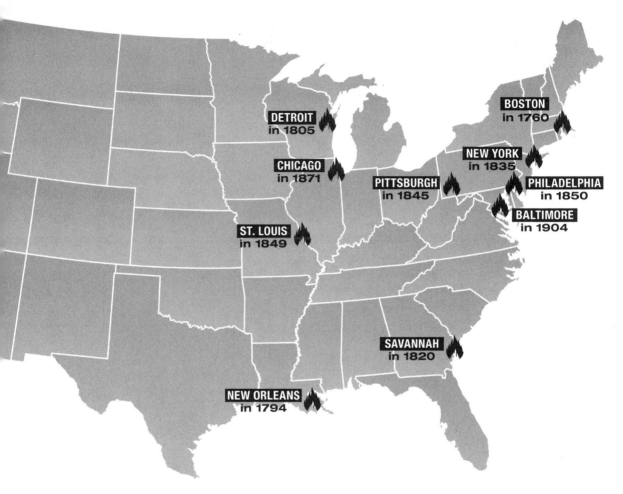

FIRE DESTROYED THESE CITIES:

DETROIT
in 1805

BOSTON
in 1760

NEW YORK
in 1835

CHICAGO
in 1871

PITTSBURGH
in 1845

PHILADELPHIA
in 1850

BALTIMORE
in 1904

ST. LOUIS
in 1849

SAVANNAH
in 1820

NEW ORLEANS
in 1794

took some 1,500 firefighters about five weeks to fully contain the blaze.

The following chapters show the destructive nature of fire through ten of the deadliest fires in American history. The challenges of firefighting have changed as our country has grown and modernized, but over the centuries these major fires have taught us valuable lessons that help prevent fires and save lives.

COLONIAL AMERICA'S BIGGEST FIRE

BOSTON, 1760

In the days of Benjamin Franklin and George Washington, big fires regularly destroyed towns and cities, but no city burned more than Boston.

Between Boston's founding in 1630 and the start of the American Revolution in 1775, fires regularly devastated large sections of the city. It's not hard to see why. The Puritans who settled on Boston's hilly Shawmut Peninsula used wood from nearby forests to build practically everything—houses, churches, and shops. They even used it to make chimneys. And the colonists cooked meals and heated their homes with open fireplaces full of wood crackling and popping. At night, candles and oil lamps provided light.

Colonial Boston had its first recorded fire in 1631, when a chimney caught fire and burned a house down. Soon afterward the colonies had their first fire code: "noe man shall build his chimney with wood, nor cover his house with thatch." New regulations followed each big fire. Boston's Board of Selectmen, which was like a city council, required residents to clean their chimneys regularly. The selectmen also decreed that "no dwelling house in Boston shall be erected and set up except of stone or brick and covered with slate or tyle."

In 1678, the selectmen purchased the latest firefighting equipment, an English-made "hand tub fire engine." At the time the word *engine* simply meant a tool or instrument. It was a rectangular wooden vessel with a pump, a short leather hose, and handles on each side for carrying. During a fire, a line of men, women, and children, which was called a bucket brigade, drew buckets of water from a creek or well and passed them to firefighters to fill the engine. Several men pumped the engine while one held the hose, which spurted water 15 to 20 feet.

The selectmen chose a dozen men to operate the

One of the first fire engines used in North America. [LOC, USZ62-99616]

engine. The man in charge was called the engineer. They were paid for each fire they fought, which gives Boston its claim to having had America's first paid firefighters.

Some twenty Bostonians in 1718 organized a mutual fire society, pledging to help one another if a fire started in their homes or shops. The rules required that "each Member confidently keep together in good Order in his Dwelling House, Two Leather Buckets, a Bed Winch, and two Bags." During a fire, the society's members filled their bags with dishes, clothing, and other small items. With the winches, they dismantled beds, often a family's most valuable possessions.

Benjamin Franklin was born in Boston, and at age five he witnessed the Great Fire of 1711, which destroyed some one hundred buildings in the center of town. In 1736, as an adult living in Philadelphia, Franklin helped to organize America's first

Benjamin Franklin organized the first volunteer firefighting company. [LOC, USZ62-45191]

volunteer fire company, the Union Fire Company. Franklin's firefighters were "Brave men, men of Spirit and Humanity, good Citizens or Neighbours, capable and worthy of civil society, and the Enjoyment of a happy Government." Boston and other colonial cities soon organized their own volunteer fire companies.

As in Philadelphia, Boston's volunteers included the town's leading citizens. "It is of some Importance in Boston," noted John Adams, America's second president, "to belong to a Fire Clubb and to choose and get admitted to a good one." Many Bostonians who distinguished themselves in the American Revolution, such as Samuel Adams, John Hancock, and Paul Revere, were volunteer firefighters.

Boston also organized nighttime street patrols or fire watches. This practice dated back to ancient Rome, when men on night patrol were called "vigils" because they were vigilant, or watchful. Time is of the essence when fighting a fire. By discovering a blaze quickly, alerting residents, and summoning firefighters, vigilant patrols saved property and lives.

In the spring of 1760, Boston's population of fifteen thousand people made it the third-largest city in the colonies. In addition to its building codes,

*This eighteenth-century print depicts a bucket brigade
filling an engine with water.* [LOC, DIG-ppmsca-01574]

mutual societies, and night watchmen, the city had nine fire engines and about one hundred volunteer fire-fighters. The city appeared prepared but wasn't.

The regulations requiring that dwellings and shops be built of brick or stone had never been strictly enforced. Many buildings along the narrow, winding streets in the oldest part of Boston were wood. In fact, wood was everywhere. Stacks of logs for heating and cooking sat beside every house and shop. Plus, bakers, blacksmiths, brewers, coopers, and tanners kept piles of logs for their ovens and furnaces.

Little rain had fallen for several weeks, so all of this combustible material was especially dry. Making conditions worse, a strong March wind blew across the peninsula.

At 3:00 A.M. on Thursday, March 20, a watchman saw flames in the Brazen Head Tavern and Inn on Pudding Lane in Cornhill, a neighborhood between the Boston Common and the harbor. The fire probably started when embers popped out of the inn's fireplace. Summoned by church bells, firefighters carrying ladders and buckets and pulling engines, which were now on wheels, ran to Pudding Lane.

In 1775, George Washington gave this engine to the new Friendship Fire Company of Alexandria, Virginia. [LOC, USZ62-12289]

Unable to save the Brazen Head, the men tried to stop the fire from spreading.

The firefighters threw water on neighboring buildings and used their hooks and chains to pull down several shops and homes to create a firebreak. A firebreak is an open space cleared as much as possible of flammable material. The demolished buildings also made it easier for firefighters to soak the rubble and extinguish firebrands as these airborne embers landed. But that night, nothing worked.

A sailor from Nova Scotia named David Perry described the scene in his journal: "While we were here the town took fire in the night . . . the wind in the north-west and pretty high; and in spite of all we could do with the engines, &c. it spread a great way down King's Street, and went across and laid all that part of the town in ashes, down to Fort Hill. We attended through the whole, and assisted in carrying water to the engines."

The inferno lit up the sky. People sixty miles north of Boston reported seeing the red glow. By dawn, the fire was "a perfect torrent of flame," recalled Bostonian William Cooper. "It is not easy to describe the Terror of that Fatal morning. . . . The distressed Inhabitants of those Buildings wrapped in Fire scarce knew where to take refuge."

At the harbor, about half a mile from where it

started, the fire burned Hallowell's Shipyard and Wendell's Wharf, where a storehouse full of gunpowder exploded. The blaze destroyed one sailing ship and damaged nine others before burning out at the water's edge.

Surprisingly, no one died. "In the midst of our Distress we have great cause for Thanksgiving," Cooper wrote, "that not withstanding the rage of the fire, the explosion at the Small Battery, and the falling of the walls, and chimneys, Divine Providence, who so mercifully ordered it, not one life has been lost and few wounded."

But the rest of the news wasn't good. The "Great Fire of 1760" was the worst fire of the colonial era. In ten hours, the fire had destroyed 349 buildings, mostly in the South End. Because of the wind's direction, the Meeting House was spared. Many protests a few years later against British policies, such as the Boston Tea Party, began at the Old South Meeting House.

Prominent Bostonians offered explanations for the fire that might seem odd to reasonable people today but were widely believed then. The Reverend Jonathan Mayhew, the man later credited with coining the phrase "no taxation without representation,"

The Old South Meeting House survived the fire of 1760 and an even larger fire in 1872. [Boston Public Library]

gave his "Sermon Occasioned by the Great Fire" at Old West Church on Cambridge Street. Mayhew told his congregation:

> *But it seems that God, who had spared us before beyond our hopes, was now determined to let loose his wrath upon us, to rebuke us in his anger, and chasten us in his hot displeasure. . . . Soon after the fire broke out, he caused his wind to blow; and suddenly raised it to such a height, that all endeavors to put a stop to the raging flames, were ineffectual.*

Why was God angry? Because Bostonians were skipping church and "profaning" the Sabbath by working.

Despite believing that mortal men couldn't prevent destructive

Paul Revere's print eight years after the Great Fire shows British ships of war arriving in Boston Harbor. [LOC, USZ62-134241]

fires, the selectmen became tougher about enforcing building codes—especially the ones requiring that new houses and shops be made of brick or stone, with tile or slate roofs. The city widened and straightened narrow streets that would act as firebreaks and give firefighters more room to maneuver. It also bought more ladders and dug new wells.

But these improvements did little to help the Great Fire's victims. The blaze had destroyed the wooden tenements of free African Americans and the brick homes of wealthy merchants. Once-prosperous families were penniless and homeless. Carpenters, coopers, and coppersmiths had lost their tools and couldn't earn a living. Fire insurance, which would have helped them replace their property, wasn't common at that time. Other colonies and merchants in England sent money and goods, but not enough.

Boston's selectmen wrote a letter to King George and to Parliament in London, asking "most humbly . . . to take their calamities case into their compassionate consideration, and grant them such relief as to the great wisdom and goodness of this Honorable House shall deem proper." Two years later, the selectmen received a reply. The letter simply stated their request had been received, but no aid was offered.

Some historians have wondered if the Great Fire of 1760 added to the grievances that led to the American Revolution. Already frustrated by Parliament's and the king's indifference to their plight, Bostonians grew angrier when Britain imposed the Sugar Act of 1764, the Stamp Act of 1765, and other new taxes. Their resentment led to a revolution, which began on April 19, 1775, at the Battles of Lexington and Concord.

A TERRIBLE TORRENT OF FIRE

NEW YORK, 1835

"How shall I record the events of last night, or how to attempt to describe the most awful calamity which has ever visited the United States?" former New York mayor Phillip Hone wrote after his city's big fire the week before Christmas. "I am fatigued in body, disturbed in mind, and my fancy filled with images of horror which my pen is inadequate to describe."

The weather, as people in Boston knew all too well, often plays an important role in major fires. It's hard to imagine a worse time for a fire than December 16 and 17, 1835. "The night was bitterly cold—seventeen degrees below zero," an eyewitness named

William Callender wrote, "and the wind blew a hurricane."

At about 9:00 P.M. that Friday, William Hayes, a watchman patrolling the streets of lower Manhattan, smelled smoke. He summoned other watchmen and they traced the smoke to the five-story Comstock & Adams hardware store on Merchant Street, near where the East River meets New York Harbor.

"We managed to force open the door," Hayes said later. "We found the whole interior of the building in flames from cellar to roof and I can tell you we shut that door mighty quick. Almost immediately the flames broke through the roof. It was the most awful night I ever saw."

That building was in the wholesale dry goods and hardware district, where merchants who supplied shops in New York and other cities stored merchandise such as tea, coffee, dresses, lace, hats, and lead. The district's six- and seven-story brick warehouses had iron shutters on the windows to keep out thieves. And they had copper roofs, which wouldn't catch fire if firebrands from a nearby burning building landed on them. This night would test just how well those safeguards worked.

This print shows firemen in the nineteenth century pulling an engine to a fire. [LOC, USZC4-6029]

A watchman alerted the fire sentinel stationed in the cupola atop City Hall. The sentinel rang a big iron bell to summon volunteer firefighters. He signaled the burning building's location by the number of peals and by hanging a lantern on the side of the cupola facing the fire. Church bells and fire-bell towers across the city repeated the alarm.

New York City, occupying just lower Manhattan Island at that time, had a population of 300,000 people. After the Erie Canal opened in 1825, New York had become the center of American commerce and business. Its 98-year-old volunteer fire department was one of the country's biggest and best trained. Unlike Philadelphia's and Boston's blue-blooded firefighters, New York's fifteen hundred volunteers weren't prominent citizens, but working-class men. They served under full-time fire chief "Handsome Jim" Gulick.

The department's equipment included 49 water-pump engines, called pumpers, with names such as Eagle 13, Oceanus, Black Joke, Old Honey Bee, and Lady Washington. The pump engine was a recent innovation. It didn't need to be filled by buckets of water. The pump had a suction hose to draw water from a well, cistern, or other source. The department also had five hose carts and six hook and ladder carts. Responding to fires, the men pulled their carts and dashed through the streets at breakneck speeds.

Volunteer firefighters, unlike today's professionals, didn't sleep at their firehouses. When an alarm sounded, they had to run to their stations and grab their equipment. It took the first company, Engine No. 1, ten minutes to reach Merchant Street.

Wells provided New York's water, but that night they were frozen solid. The firefighters had to chop holes in the ice covering the East River. Then they connected hoses from pumper to pumper. Black Joke Engine Company No. 33 drew water from the river and pumped it to Chatham Engine

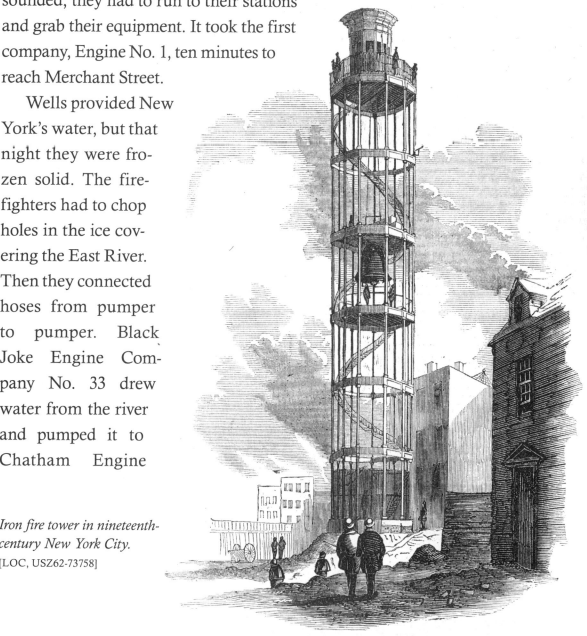

Iron fire tower in nineteenth-century New York City.
[LOC, USZ62-73758]

Company No. 2, which pumped it to Engine Company No. 13, nearly four hundred feet from the river. But before the water reached the nozzleman at the end of the hose, it turned to icy slush. Without water, the firefighters could do little and the fire quickly spread.

The flames in the warehouses, recalled volunteer firefighter Gabriel O. Disoway, made the closed iron shutters shine "with glowing redness, until at last forced open by the uncontrollable enemy. Within, they represented the appearance of an immense iron furnace in full blast." The heat exceeded 2,000 degrees Fahrenheit, melting shutters and copper roofs.

Nathaniel Currier's lithograph of the first night of the big blaze sold thousands of copies in just a few days.
[LOC, USZ62-2553]

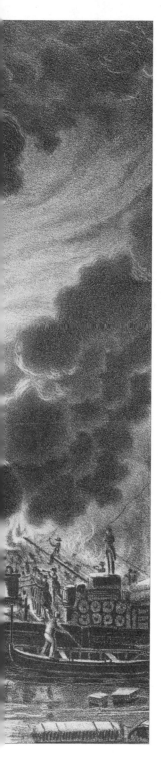

By 12:30 A.M., the wind had driven the fire north to Wall Street. Then, as now, it was the heart of New York's business district. "I stood at the corner of Wall and Pearl Street, where there is an open space like a funnel," William Callender recalled. "The fire in great sheets of flame leaped across that space, cavorting around in maddening fury."

Confident that the new three-story marble Merchants' Exchange wouldn't burn, people filled it with merchandise saved from burning warehouses and stores. But soon the Merchants' Exchange as well as the nearby post office, banks, and churches were ablaze. "Street after street caught the terrible torrent," observed writer Augustine E. Costello, "until acre after acre was booming an ocean of flame."

A lithograph by Nathaniel Currier showing a view of the great fire from the water. [LOC, USZ62-50387]

Thousands of rowdy people watched. Two were killed. One person burned to death, and a mob lynched a man caught setting a fire. While many citizens helped firefighters, some stole hats, wine, and other merchandise that was piled in the streets. The police arrested three hundred people for looting. The less ambitious got drunk on stolen liquor and cheered the spectacular fire.

Turpentine stored in burning warehouses by the river exploded. "The water looked like a sea of blood," wrote Costello. "Clouds of smoke, like dark mountains suddenly rising in the air, were succeeded by long banners of flame."

Mayor Cornelius Lawrence was worried the blaze would spread north of Wall Street to the residential neighborhoods. A firebreak, he decided, might stop it. Sailors and marines from the Brooklyn Navy Yard, across the East River, used kegs of gunpowder to blow up several buildings on Exchange Place. The firebreak worked. But below Wall Street, the blaze lasted eight more hours, dying only when nothing was left to burn.

The city's financial and commercial district—674 buildings on 17 city blocks—was smoldering rubble. "The heart of the city seemed to have ceased to exist," observed Costello. "Of business there was none. New York was stricken as with paralysis."

The estimated financial loss was as high as forty million dollars. That would be about one billion dollars in today's money. Unable to pay all the claims, 23 of the city's 26 fire insurance companies went bankrupt. Without insurance money to replace losses, many other businesses failed. By destroying

This is a painting by the Italian-born artist Nicolino Calyo, an eyewitness to the fire. [New York City Fire Museum]

the center of American commerce, some historians believe, New York's Great Fire of 1835 added to the economic problems that a year later caused the worst recession the young nation had experienced.

City officials and insurance companies wanted a reliable water supply to make New York safer. Construction of the Croton Water System began in 1837. Five years and twelve million dollars later, New York had the world's biggest, most modern water system. Some 35 million gallons of water a day from reservoirs 41 miles north of the city flowed through iron pipes to fortress-like receiving reservoirs on Manhattan Island. The Croton Water System, like the Erie Canal before it and the Brooklyn Bridge after it, was one of the nineteenth century's great engineering feats.

A Currier & Ives depiction of New York several years after the fire. [LOC, DIG-pga-03183]

AMERICA'S MOST FAMOUS FIRE

CHICAGO, 1871

Unlike New York City 36 years earlier, Chicago had a state-of-the-art water system when America's most famous fire began on October 8, 1871.

That Sunday evening, Robert A. Williams, the Chicago Fire Department's 43-year-old chief marshal, was getting some much-needed sleep. Earlier, he and his entire department of 185 firemen had spent 16 hours battling a lumber mill fire that destroyed four city blocks. His men were not only tired but also hurting from swollen eyes, blistered skin, and lungs raw from breathing heat and smoke. Williams had been in bed only a couple of hours when, just after 9:00 P.M., his wife woke him with news of another fire.

It had started in a barn behind Catherine and Patrick O'Leary's home at 137 DeKoven Street. There was a popular belief that a cow had kicked over a kerosene lantern. Mrs. O'Leary did keep a cow so that she could sell milk, but that urban myth has been discredited. In fact, no one knows how the fire began. Some people suspect a smoker passing by carelessly tossed a lit cigarette into the hay.

A neighbor discovered the blaze and alerted the O'Learys. More neighbors helped save the family's furniture. Nearly thirty minutes passed before someone thought to turn in a fire alarm.

A Chicago Fire Department (CFD) sentinel downtown in the courthouse cupola spotted the smoke. But he assumed the smoke was coming from the smoldering mill fire, which had been near the O'Leary home, and didn't report it.

Chicago, which residents called "the Gem of the Prairie," was the biggest city in the Midwest. In just four decades, it had burgeoned from a frontier settlement of a few hundred people along Lake Michigan to a metropolis of some 300,000. Residents built

Chicago's State Street was one of the world's busiest thoroughfares in the nineteenth century. [Chicago History Museum]

homes and stores with cheap, plentiful lumber from nearby Wisconsin forests. Along Lake Michigan's marshy shore, they even laid 55 miles of pine-board streets and 600 miles of pine-board sidewalks.

In the downtown business district, now known as the Loop, many of the new buildings were said to be fireproof. They included the two-year-old limestone and iron Water Works Pumping Station. It was part of a new water system that, like New York's, had been an engineering feat.

Back in 1864, Chicago's officials had decided the water along the shore was too polluted for the city's residents. Hundreds of Irish immigrant workers began digging a five-foot-wide tunnel thirty feet beneath the bottom of Lake Michigan; it would stretch two miles from shore in order to supply fresh water to the city. Using only picks and shovels, the workers labored around the clock six days a week for nearly three years. They completed the Lake Tunnel in 1867, and two years later they finished the Water Works Pumping Station and its 15-story tower, one of the city's tallest structures.

Chicago also had installed street call boxes. Fire-prone Boston had installed the first ones in the early 1850s. The small house-shaped boxes were mounted on poles throughout the city. To report a fire, a person pulled a lever, which sent a telegraph signal to the Chicago Fire Department (CFD) and indicated the fire's location.

The CFD also had horse-drawn steam engines that could shoot six hundred gallons of water a minute as far as two-thirds the length of a football field. English inventors half a century earlier had built the first steam-powered fire engines, but it took years to make them reliable. A company in Cincinnati, Ohio, made one of the first successful American models. That 22,000-pound engine, named Uncle Joe Ross, pumped water through six hoses.

Cities that bought these expensive engines wanted them operated by trained full-time firefighters, so they replaced volunteers with paid professionals. Cincinnati formed the nation's first professional department in 1853. Five years later, Chicago's City Council created the CFD. But the council pinched pennies when it came to funding. The 185 full-time firefighters weren't enough for the sprawling city. The CFD wanted more fireboats on the Chicago River, which was lined by lumberyards, coal yards, warehouses, and wharves. And it also wanted building inspectors, because poorly constructed and maintained structures were fire threats.

But the business community opposed raising taxes to pay for a bigger fire department. It also

FRANK LESLIE'S
ILLUSTRATED
NEWSPAPER

Entered according to the Act of Congress, in the year 1871, by FRANK LESLIE, in the office of the Librarian of Congress, at Washington.

No. 839—VOL. XXXIII.]   NEW YORK, OCTOBER 28, 1871.   [PRICE, 10 CENTS. $4 00 YEARLY. 13 WEEKS, $1 00.

THE GREAT FIRE AT CHICAGO.—SCENE IN WELLS STREET—THE TERRIFIED POPULACE IN FRONT OF THE BRIGGS HOUSE, WHICH HAS JUST CAUGHT FIRE.—FROM A SKETCH BY OUR SPECIAL ARTIST.—SEE PAGE 102.

opposed stricter building codes that would make new construction more expensive. This shortsightedness, it turned out, was costly.

By the time Chief Marshal Williams arrived at the fire on the night of October 8, two blocks of the crowded Irish immigrant neighborhood were in flames. Little rain had fallen in three months, so everything was bone-dry. Only the men with the engines America and Little Giant had turned out, which is a fireman's phrase meaning *responded.* Williams immediately sent a second alarm, requesting more engines.

The chief marshal positioned his men and pumpers around the burning houses, and they sprayed thousands of gallons of water on the flames. Just as the fire appeared to be under control, a southwesterly wind picked up and fanned the flames higher.

As the inferno grew, the heat radiated hundreds of feet, causing trees and buildings to burst into flame. The strong updraft created a wind, or convection current, called a firestorm. "The wind had increased to a tempest," a resident recalled, "and hurled great blazing brands over our heads." Five

When an artist in St. Louis heard about the Chicago fire, he rushed to the Illinois city by train. His sketches are among the few by an eyewitness. [LOC, USZ62-109590]

blocks from the O'Leary home, airborne embers ignited the steeple on St. Paul's Roman Catholic Church. More firebrands, like tiny paratroopers of an invading army, floated down onto lumberyards and furniture factories. At 10:30, Williams turned in a third alarm, bringing out all the CFD's 15 steam fire engines.

Beyond the church was the 400-foot-wide South Branch of the Chicago River. The intense heat ignited the coal yards and lumberyards along the river and burned boats and barges. Flames even danced on the water, which was covered by grease, oil, and other industrial waste. Soon buildings across the river were ablaze.

With the fire spreading so rapidly, Chief Marshal Williams desperately wanted more men and equipment. Mayor Roswell B. Mason telegraphed St. Louis, Milwaukee, Dayton, Fort Wayne, and other nearby cities. "CHICAGO IS IN FLAMES," read his message to Milwaukee's mayor. "SEND YOUR WHOLE DEPARTMENT TO HELP US."

Across the South Branch, the inferno spread to Conley's Patch, a neighborhood of German, Irish, and Scandinavian immigrants. It burned the Gas Works, where, fortunately, workers had shut down the pipes to prevent an explosion.

Flames leaping high in the air swept downtown, engulfing the city's best-known buildings—the Chamber of Commerce, the Chicago Times Building, the Chicago Academy of Music, Crosby's Opera House, the post office, the Custom House, Booksellers' Row, the Palmer Hotel, and Marshall Field's, a six-story department store dubbed "the marble palace," which occupied a whole city block.

The 10,849-pound brass bell in the cupola atop the new limestone courthouse swayed in the wind, ringing nonstop. After the interior of the courthouse caught fire, the guard in the basement jail released the 160 prisoners, telling them to run for their lives. Minutes later, its supports weakened by fire, the brass bell plunged through five floors to the basement. The impact thundered across the city.

"Suddenly there came a crash like a broadside of artillery," said Samuel S. Greeley, who was watching from the roof of his home north of downtown, "and a vast jet of smoke and sparks shot to heaven. It almost seemed to me, at nearly a mile away, that I felt the earth tremble."

Like many onlookers at big fires, Greeley was mesmerized. "The scene was now indescribably grand and awful. In the half hour that I had passed upon my roof, the fire had leaped forward with

MAP
OF
CHICAGO;
SHOWING THE
Parks, Boulevards,
AND
Burnt District,
ACCOMPANYING
CHICAGO
AND THE
Great Conflagration,
BY
COLBERT & CHAMBERLIN.

frightful speed, and was beginning to break out in detached spots in advance of the terrible mass. The wind had risen, and was now blowing almost a gale; the masses of floating fire from roofs and warehouses were more numerous, and more fiery, and the roar of flames and of falling walls was more appalling."

Soon the fire jumped the Chicago River's North Branch and invaded the neighborhoods where Greeley and 75,000 other people lived. Few residents had begun evacuating because they didn't think the blaze would spread so far so fast. Suddenly, the streets became "a torrent of humanity," one man said, "gorged with horses pulling wagons piled high with furniture. Mobs of men and women rushed wildly from street to street screaming, gesticulating and shouting."

One of the main avenues, a visiting New Yorker later wrote, "was utterly choked with all manner of goods and people. . . . Valuable oil paintings, books, pet animals, musical instruments, toys, mirrors, and bedding, were trampled under foot."

While many people raced to the city's outskirts, an estimated thirty thousand found refuge in one of

This map shows the vast section of Chicago destroyed by the fire. [LOC, USZ62-67787]

[NEXT PAGE] *A Currier & Ives depiction of the fire from Lake Michigan.* [LOC, DIG-pga-00762]

CORNER
TE & MADISON ST
TER CHICAGO FIRE

the few open spaces down-town: Lincoln Park, along Lake Michigan. "In some instances whole families were huddled around their little piles of furniture, which was all they had left," Judge Lambert Tree recalled. "Here and there a mother sat upon the ground clinging to her infant, with one or more little ones, who, exhausted by the prolonged interruptions to their slumbers, were now sleeping." A number of people spent the night standing in the cold lake.

All hope was lost when, at 3:00 A.M. on Monday, the firefighters' hoses went limp. Sparks had fallen through the Water Works building's ventilators, setting the

After the fire, State Street was no longer one of the world's busiest streets. [Chicago History Museum]

interior ablaze and causing the roof to collapse onto the water pumps. The fire continued burning, reaching Division Street, a mile north of the river, until it began to rain that evening.

No one had seen such destruction since the Civil War, which had ended six years earlier. "Heaps of ruins and here and there a standing wall, as far as the eye could reach," a resident wrote. The fire burned a swath through the city three-quarters of a mile wide and four miles long. A third of the population, 100,000 people, was homeless. Officials believed some 300 people died, but they found the remains of only 120. The city lost 17,500 buildings, nearly a third of the 59,500 structures standing the previous week. The financial loss was a staggering $222 million, which would be about $4 billion today.

Some losses were priceless. The fire destroyed the

A panoramic view of the destruction. [LOC, USZC4-9440]

Chicago Historical Society. Its treasures included Abraham Lincoln's original Emancipation Proclamation.

Despite the widespread devastation, the city rebuilt quickly. Workers shoveled the bricks, limestone, and other rubble into Lake Michigan as landfill. Residents hastily put up

The O'Leary home, where the Great Chicago Fire began, didn't burn because of the prevailing winds.
[LOC, USZ62-57060]

A mid-twentieth-century cartoon showing Mrs. O'Leary's cow imagining a city of skyscrapers as she intentionally kicks over the lantern. [LOC, DIG-ppmsca-09127]

wooden homes and stores. A few years later, a new style of structure appeared that changed skylines around the world.

The world's first steel-framed skyscraper—the ten-story Home Insurance Building in downtown Chicago—was finished in 1885. By the end of the century, Chicago was becoming a city of steel skyscrapers. It even inspired a style of modern architecture known as the Chicago School.

Today, the Chicago Fire Academy stands where the O'Leary barn once stood. And each year the nation is reminded of Chicago's Great Fire because National Fire Prevention Week is observed the week of October 8.

NEW CENTURY, OLD PROBLEM

BALTIMORE, 1904

For centuries, people thought the fires that regularly laid waste to cities were unavoidable. But by the beginning of the twentieth century, electric lights, combustion engines, telephones, and other innovations were making life easier. It seemed that the science and technology that made these possible would also make fire less of a threat.

In 1904, Baltimore, Maryland, with a population of 500,000 people, was America's sixth-largest city. Ships from all over the world filled its busy harbor. In the nearby central business district, skyscrapers cast shadows over colonial-era churches and row houses. Daniel Burnham, a famous Chicago School architect, had designed Baltimore's tallest structure, the 16-story Continental Trust Building. This and the other steel and concrete buildings had the latest fire safeguards, such as automatic alarms connected to the Baltimore City Fire Department and automatic sprinklers, which were patented soon after the Great Chicago Fire. Several of the new structures were supposed to be fireproof.

Baltimore had relied on volunteer firefighters for more than a century. By the 1850s, volunteer companies there and in other cities had become warring gangs, skirmishing in the streets, burning one another's engine houses, and even battling over who got to fight a fire. An official in Cincinnati called his city's volunteer fire companies "nurseries where the youth of the city are trained in vice, vulgarity, and debauchery." Wanting more reliable service, Baltimore created a full-time professional fire department in 1858.

But like Chicago years earlier, the growing Maryland seaport hadn't invested enough money in fire prevention. It needed a better water supply. And in the densely populated business district, hydrants were old and few, which became a big problem on February 7, 1904.

On that cold Sunday, the alarm from John E. Hurst & Company's wholesale dry goods building

CHIEF BELT. BREAKS ALL RECORDS
FROM CAMDEN STATION, TO SCENE
OF FIRE AT BALTO.

*The Washington, D.C., fire chief rushing from the
train station to the fire.* [LOC, DIG-npcc-18727]

downtown on German Street sounded at Baltimore City Fire Department (BCFD) headquarters at 10:48 A.M. The men of Engine Company No. 15 turned out, wearing heavy coats to keep them dry and insulated from heat and hard leather helmets to protect them from falling debris.

When Captain John Kahl and the firefighters of Engine Company No. 15 broke into the six-story Hurst Building, they saw smoke coming from the wood-frame elevator shaft. Captain Kahl also noticed a layer of smoke spreading across the ceiling, which indicated a possible "flashover." This happens when intense heat causes flammable material to produce gas that explodes into a ball of flame. The firefighters quickly left, and minutes later a ground-shaking explosion, perhaps caused by drums of gasoline stored in the building's basement, shattered windows and scattered burning debris. The captain immediately turned in second and third alarms.

One problem for early-twentieth-century firefighters was the thicket of electric and telegraph wires strung above the narrow downtown streets. The wires made it hard to maneuver tall ladders. And debris falling from burning buildings snapped

The scene near the Hurst Building just a few minutes after the fire began. [LOC, USZ62-45622]

wires, which could electrocute firefighters on the ground. An hour after the fire began, a downed electric wire sent Fire Chief George Horton to the hospital.

The district fire chief, August Emrich, and Baltimore's 36-year-old mayor, Robert McLane, took command. "We're in God's Hands," Chief Emrich said. "The winds are too much for us and there is not enough water in Baltimore to keep those flames from spreading."

The fire quickly engulfed seven blocks of warehouses and offices. As often happens in big fires, the intense heat created a firestorm. "Throughout the terrible contest which firemen and fire waged for supremacy,"

Downtown Baltimore engulfed in flames and smoke. [LOC, USZ62-45624]

wrote a *New York Times* reporter, "humanity was handicapped by a gale which carried burning brands far over the heads of the workers and beyond the reach of the hundreds of streams of water poured into the raging furnaces."

The flames, the *Times* reported, "sent their fierce tongues 200 feet into the air, which filled the heavens first with a pall of black funereal smoke, and then with livid sheets of spark and lurid cinders. . . . Buildings sprang into living flame before fire touched them, and brick and stone and mortar crumbled like chalk. The atmosphere quivered, and in it, surrounded by fire, the firemen fought doggedly."

The BCFD tried to stay in front of the fire, but the wind kept changing directions, sending firefighters scrambling from one side of downtown to another as they fought to keep the flames from invading surrounding residential neighborhoods.

Business owners and their employees hastily tried to save their important records by loading them into wagons and pushcarts. But workers in the Equitable Building didn't see the need to remove records or themselves from their offices. They said their building was fireproof. Fortunately, officials persuaded them to leave before the heat shattered the windows and the Equitable's interior burned like kindling.

The inferno attracted hundreds of spectators,

who were described by a newspaper account: "Great multitudes of people line the streets, awestruck with the dazzling but grewsome panorama which is being enacted before their eyes." To control the crowds, the governor called out one thousand Maryland National Guardsmen. But bystanders were orderly and hundreds helped firefighters by forming bucket brigades and by extinguishing firebrands.

Within an hour after the fire began, firefighters from Harrisburg, Wilmington, and other neighboring cities began to arrive. Firefighters from Washington, D.C.—about forty miles south of Baltimore—traveled by train and arrived first. One fireman recalled that as they pulled into Baltimore, "we knew then that we were heading for something big. I think we all got a little scared."

The out-of-town firefighters had a hard time getting their equipment through streets crowded by onlookers and debris. Then they discovered their hoses didn't fit Baltimore's fire hydrants. They had to use strips of canvas to bind hose and hydrant couplings, which worked, but resulted in less water pressure.

Despite the equipment problems, bitter cold, and strong winds, "the great army of firefighters performed many daring feats in their desperate attempt to stay the flames," the *Times* reported. "Many times they were driven out of close and hot places just as

A damaged fire ladder wagon.
[LOC, DIG-npcc-18724]

walls came toppling down." But daring feats weren't enough. By nightfall, seven hours after it started, the fire had razed 30 acres.

Mayor McLane decided to try the age-old technique of creating firebreaks. Explosive specialists put hundreds of sticks of dynamite inside the Schwab Bros. Building, the John Duer and Son Building, and the Armstrong Shoe Company. But the blasts didn't topple the structures. They only made the fire worse by breaking windows in nearby buildings and scattering flaming debris.

The *Times* described the burning city as though it were a Fourth of July fireworks spectacle:

During all of these hours the pyrotechnic display has been magnificent and imposing beyond the power of [a] painter to depict . . . vast columns of seething flame are shooting skyward at varying points of the compass, and the firmament is one vast prismatic ocean of golden and silver hued sparks.

Late that night, the 30-mile-per-hour winds shifted and pushed the fire to the southeast. This shift spared City Hall and the courthouse, along with the important legal records they held, but it doomed part of the harbor's two miles of wharves and warehouses. About two hundred oyster boats under sail, a reporter wrote, resembled "a flock of great white fowl as they swept down the harbor in a closely packed bunch" to escape the flames. After anchoring their boats safely in the outer harbor, the oystermen returned to help firefighters.

Three big Norwegian steamers loaded with tropical fruit weren't as nimble. The fast-paced fire reached the wharf while the ships were still docked there. In the nick of time, two tugboats, the *Oriole* and the *Meta*, raced across the harbor, hitched their hawsers, which are thick ropes, to the steamers, and pulled them to safety.

The fire also trapped a fruit company president and his employees, who were removing business records from their warehouse. The men ran to the end of the wharf, thinking their only hope was to swim across the harbor. But the *Oriole* once again came to the rescue.

For a while, the flames threatened Federal Hill, a neighborhood south of the inner harbor. But Philadelphia and Baltimore firefighters held them back until the wind shifted again, pushing the fire toward the lumberyards and the Russian and Polish immigrant neighborhoods of East Baltimore.

On Monday morning, an army of 1,200 firefighters and 37 steam-powered fire engines battled the fire along Jones Falls, a 75-foot-wide foul-smelling stream dividing downtown from East Baltimore. "Again and again the terrible heat was driven from the burning district across Jones Falls and ignited buildings and lumber piles," a newspaper reported. "Furious hand-to-hand fights occurred, which, fortunately for the residents of East Baltimore, were won by the firemen. . . . Had the fire gained a foothold in the east side lumber yards . . . nothing could have stopped the onslaught, and the departments would have been powerless to prevent damage as great as, if not greater than, that of the Chicago fire."

By 5:00 P.M. on Monday, after thirty hours, the fight was over except for "overhauling" the debris to make sure no embers or hot spots could flare up again. The *Times* described the aftermath: "Where at Saturday's close of business stood stately office structures, substantial buildings of business, and docks teeming with the shipping trade of the world there are now piles of broken brick and stone and tottering walls."

The fire sent some two hundred firefighters to the hospital suffering from burns, scalding, lacerations, and smoke inhalation. A fireman and two guardsmen caught pneumonia and died. The fire claimed another victim three months later. Under strain from

After the fire, Baltimore residents toured the destruction. [LOC, USZ62-112694]

A panorama of Baltimore's downtown after the fire. [LOC, USZ62-120267]

the work of rebuilding the city, Baltimore's young mayor killed himself.

The Great Baltimore Fire destroyed 86 city blocks and 1,526 buildings. It left 35,000 people jobless. The architects and engineers who had designed the Equitable Building and the other supposedly fireproof buildings studied the charred skeletons. One expert insisted, "to say that the structure actually burned is, of course, foolish and manifestly incorrect because they are still standing." Nonetheless, the planners returned to their drawing boards to try to design a truly fireproof building.

The Baltimore fire underscored the need to standardize firefighting equipment, especially hose couplings. According to one estimate, at the time there were over six hundred different sizes of fire-hose

couplings used throughout the country. The National Fire Protection Association encouraged cities to adopt a standard-size hydrant coupling. But few cities wanted the expense of replacing their systems. One hundred years after the Baltimore fire, only 18 of the 48 largest U.S. cities had installed hydrants meeting NFPA standards.

FIRE ON THE WATER

NEW YORK, 1904

"There was never a happier party than we were when we boarded the boat Wednesday morning," said Anna Weber, recalling her family laughing and talking the morning of June 15, before an excursion on the *General Slocum*.

Anna and her husband, two children, and six other relatives, all dressed in their best Sunday clothing, were joining thirteen hundred people for the St. Mark's Lutheran Church's seventeenth annual Sunday school excursion to Long Island. Many of these people attended St. Mark's and lived nearby in a small, close-knit German immigrant neighborhood on Manhattan's Lower East Side.

The *General Slocum*, a popular excursion boat owned by the Knickerbocker Steamship Company, was a white pine and oak vessel three stories tall and 250 feet long. It had three decks—the lower main deck, the middle promenade deck, and the open-air hurricane deck, a nautical term for a steamboat's breezy top deck. In the middle of the ship, a pair of tall pale yellow smokestacks pointed skyward. And on each side, paddle wheels 35 feet in diameter pushed the ship through the water at a top speed of about 15 knots, or about 17 miles per hour.

After the *Slocum* pulled away from the Third Street dock, it steamed up the wide East River between Manhattan and Brooklyn. At the stern, or back, of the promenade deck, a seven-piece band led by George J. Maurer

The General Slocum *was a popular New York excursion ship.*
[Mariners' Museum]

played popular German and American songs such as "Vienna Swallows" and "Swanee River." The passengers, a third of whom were age twenty or younger,

OPENING DAY — N.Y. SCHOOLS   486-7

New York City schoolchildren similar to those who perished on the Slocum. [LOC, LC-DIG-ggbain-02319]

danced, explored the ship, or leaned on the wooden railing, waving at people onshore.

Since the *Slocum* was launched 13 years earlier, William Van Schaick had been its captain. In the pilothouse on the promenade deck, Captain Van Schaick watched his two pilots steer the vessel toward Hell Gate, where the river channel narrowed and the currents were treacherous. As the *Slocum* steamed ahead at top speed, a boy appeared in the pilothouse doorway and interrupted the captain's concentration.

The 12-year-old passenger, Frank Perditsky, told the captain there was a fire on the lower deck. "Get the hell out of here and mind your own business!" Captain Van Schaick yelled, thinking this was a prank. The captain then turned his attention back to the river.

Meanwhile, a deckhand named John Coakley tried to appear calm as he searched for Ed Flanagan, the *Slocum*'s first mate and the second in command. A few minutes earlier, Coakley had been drinking a beer in the saloon, when another boy told him about the smoke. Coakley traced it to a storage room in the bow, or front, of the ship. When he opened the storage room's door, a fire smoldering in hay from a packing crate leaped to life. Coakley, leaving the door open, hurried to find the first mate.

After just a couple of minutes, Flanagan, Coakley, and several other crewmen returned. By then, nourished by oxygen flowing through the open door, the flames had spread to the stairs. The men grabbed a hose connected to a standpipe, but for some reason, no water came out. This was their only attempt to put out the fire. The *Slocum*'s 22-man crew had never held fire drills or been trained for emergencies.

Passengers soon noticed something was wrong. "I saw smoke coming up a narrow gangway leading from the lower main deck," said the Reverend George C. F. Haas, St. Mark's pastor. He was with his wife, 13-year-old daughter, sister, sister-in-law, and 3-year-old nephew. "I thought at first that the smoke might be blowing that way from the galley, where I know they were preparing to cook the clam

chowder, but the smoke speedily increased in volume and I soon realized that it was something more serious."

Other passengers were having too much fun to notice. Dozens of children and their mothers had gathered for ice cream on the lower main deck, just below the pilothouse. Suddenly, "there was a roar as

This steamship beneath the Brooklyn Bridge on the East River appears to be the General Slocum. [LOC, USZ62-59950]

though a cannon had been shot off," recalled Clara Steur, one of the passengers, "and the entire bow of the boat was one sheet of flames."

Then "the flames burst out right near us," said 14-year-old John Tischner, who was eating ice cream with a friend. "Everybody seemed to be yelling 'Fire!' and I saw a lot of women with their hair and dresses burning jump into the river."

Ten minutes after discovering the blaze, First Mate Flanagan reported it to the captain. Van Schaick later explained that he started down the stairs, but "the fire drove me back. It was sweeping up from below like a tornado."

Nicholas Balser, who was with his wife, children, and several other relatives, said he "thought that the boat would put into shore at once, but it seemed fully five minutes or more before she swung inshore. By this time, the scene was terrifying."

Captain Van Schaick didn't turn the *Slocum* toward shore, he later said, for fear of spreading the fire to the oil tanks and warehouses along the river. The captain decided to beach the ship a mile upriver, on North Brother Island. It was deserted except for Riverside Hospital, an isolated facility for people with typhoid, tuberculosis, and other infectious or contagious diseases. He estimated it would take three minutes to reach the island.

As the *Slocum* raced upriver, the headwind fanned the flames toward the stern. The steamship, like many wooden vessels, had been painted with linseed oil and turpentine to keep the wood from drying out, but these combustible liquids also made the wood burn faster.

"Sheets of flame followed the roiling clouds of smoke, and the fearful rush began to the sides of the boat," said Joseph Halphusen, St. Mark's sexton. "Women and children were thrown down and trampled on. The crew offered the passengers little help. It seemed to me that the crew of the boat lost their heads—they were undisciplined, and did not do what sane men would have done to stay the panic and restore order."

The engineers kept shoveling coal into the ship's steam boiler, while the captain and pilots stayed in the pilothouse. Everyone else was on their own.

Passengers who grabbed the ship's five hundred Never-Sink life preservers soon discovered they were useless. John Kircher, who was not on the boat, related his wife's account of what happened to their youngest daughter, Elsie. "Thinking the little girl would be perfectly safe with the preserver on, she lifted her to the rail and dropped her over the side. She waited for Elsie to come up, but the child never

[NEXT PAGE] *An artist's depiction of the ship in flames.*
[Mariners' Museum]

appeared. She had sunk as though a stone were tied to her." The life preservers were old and rotten.

Several people tried to launch the ship's six life rafts, each of which would hold twenty passengers. "Unclasping my knife," Nicholas Balser said, "I slashed at the fastenings of the life rafts nearby. But they were secured by wire instead of rope." The rafts had been wired tightly to the deck so they wouldn't rattle during rough water or storms.

Few passengers could swim, but they leaped overboard anyway. "My wife and I stood together by the rail until we saw that the upper deck was about to fall upon us," said the Reverend Haas. "We saw nothing of our little girl, who had been playing with other children. My sister stood near us. None of us could swim, but when we realized that it meant certain death to remain longer on the steamer we all jumped overboard together."

The scene in the water, John Tischner remembered, was deadly, too. "Twenty would jump at once, and right on top of them twenty more would jump. Then there would be a skirmish of grabbing at heads and arms, and the fellows that could swim would be pulled down and had to fight their way up."

The newspapers were filled with stories about the General Slocum *tragedy.*
[*The World*, June 15, 1904]

WEATHER—Cloudy, warmer; Thursday fair.

BASEBALL
RACING AND SPORTS

The
 EVENING EDITION  World.

"Circulation Books Open to All."   *"Circulation Books Open to All."*

FINAL
COMPLETE BASEBALL and SPORTING
RESULTS EDITION

PRICE ONE CENT.   NEW YORK, WEDNESDAY, JUNE 15, 1904.   PRICE ONE CENT.

LIST OF SLOCUM'S DEAD
NOW MAY REACH 1,000

LIST OF THOSE KNOWN TO HAVE PERISHED

Some of the Victims Who Met Their Death on the Steamer Gen. Slocum, Which Caught Fire When Loaded with Excursionists.

REVISED LISTS OF THE DEAD, INJURED AND MISSING WILL BE FOUND IN TO-DAY'S FINAL EDITION OF THE EVENING WORLD.

The following is a list of the known dead:

M'GANN, MICHAEL, steward of the Gen. Slocum.
SCHNEIDER, Mrs. AUGUSTA, No. 222 Stanhope street, Brooklyn.
SCHNEIDER, MARY, aged eight.
SCHNEIDER, ALICE, aged five.
BURK, ____ deckhand.
HARTUNG, Mrs. MARY.
HARTUNG, LOUIS, twenty-five.
HARTUNG, HARRY fifteen.
HARTUNG, MILLIE, thirteen.
HARTUNG, CLARA, eleven.
HARTUNG, ELSIE, five.
KLINE, Mrs. No. 31 East Sixteenth street.
BALMER, Mrs. JOSEPH, aged thirty-five, No. 123 First avenue; identified by husband.
BALMER, Mrs. MARY, No. 123 First avenue.
BORGER, FLORENCE, three years old, No. 510 Putnam avenue, Brooklyn, identified by her father, William A. Bower.
KLINGLER, Mrs. EVA.
SCHWARTZ, Mrs. ANNIE.
SCHWARTZ, Mrs. LOUISA.
GRANFIRE, Mrs. No. 300 Avenue A.
GRANFIRE, ____, nine-months-old baby of Mrs. Granfire; dead in arms.
ALBRECHT, Mrs. LILLY, No. 201 East Tenth street.
KOEHLER, HARRY, Eleventh street and Fourth avenue.
STROBEL, CATHERINE, No. 325 East Sixth street.
MAYER, Mrs. LOUISE, No. 139 East Seventeenth street.
KEPPLER, IRENE, aged twelve, No. 192 First avenue, identified by father, George Keppler.
HOFFMAN, ELIZABETH, identified at Twenty-sixth street Morgue.
FICKBOLM, Mrs. MARIE, No. 91 Avenue D.
HOFFMAN, Mrs. SOPHIE, No. 77 Second avenue.
HOFFMAN, Mrs. ELIZABETH, suggested identification from receipt or bill on body.
KLEXMAN, Mrs. ____, supposed identification from inscriptions in wedding ring on body.
SMITH, MARY, festival, of No. 138 Seventh street.
SCHUMPF, Mrs. JACOB, No. 208 Avenue B.
STRINO, Mrs. AUGUSTA, fifty-two years old, of No. 90 First avenue.
ROTH, Mrs. JOSEPHINE, No. 203 Fifth street.
BEHRENS, Mrs. AUGUSTA, No. 127 Garden street, Hoboken.
BIUM, Mrs. CHRISTINA, No. 315 East Sixth street.
ABUNDIS, Mrs. MARY, No. 245 East Eighteenth street.
SCHNITZLER, Mrs. FANNIE, No. 10 Gouverneur place, Bronx.
KOBLER, HENRY, No. 208 East Thirteenth street.

34 BODIES TAKEN TO POLICE STATION.

The following is a list of the unidentified dead taken to the Alexander avenue station:

The bodies are numbered as follows:

No. 1—Woman, 4 feet 4 inches, 250 pounds, dark brown hair, black skirt, white waist, wedding ring, amber beads.
No. 2—Woman, forty years, 130 pounds, dark complexion, brown hair, 5 feet, black skirt and waist, small black flower earrings with small diamond in centre.
No. 3—Woman, sixty, 5 feet, 150 pounds, gray hair, reddish brown striped skirt and waist, no jewels.
No. 4—Woman, 30, 5 feet 5, 200 pounds, wedding ring, gold and diamond earrings, white waist, white striped black skirt.
No. 5—Woman, 25, 140 pounds, 5 feet 7, black skirt, low shoes, wedding ring, small black earrings.
No. 6—Woman, thirty-five, 5 feet 6 inches, weight 180 pounds, brown hair, brown skirt, white waist, wedding ring, diamond earrings, gold and diamond brooch. Later identified as Mrs. Mary Balmer, of No. 123 First avenue.
No. 7 Unknown woman, thirty-five 5 feet 7 inches, weight 150 pounds; light brown hair, white waist, black skirt, solitaire ring and wedding ring, diamond screw earrings.
No. 8 Woman, twenty-five, 5 feet 6 inches, weight 150 pounds; dark brown hair, white waist, black skirt, low shoes, pearl earrings, pearl and gold brooch, wedding ring, diamond ring. Eight gold ladies' watch, No. 445,130, stopped at 10.13.
No. 9 Woman, fifty, 5 feet 5 inches, 160 pounds, dark brown hair, light waist, black skirt, oxford shoes, gold and diamond earrings, small plain gold ring on right hand.
No. 10—Woman, forty-five, 5 feet 6 inches, 160 pounds, black and gray hair, black calico dress and purple flowers, wedding ring, brooch showing man's picture.
No. 11 Woman, fifty, 4 feet 2 inches, 170 pounds, dark brown hair,

GENERAL SLOCUM AFIRE AND SINKING.

From photographs taken by Photographer Curtis for The Evening World.

ESTIMATE OF DEAD, AND WHERE FOUND

Pastor Haas, of St. Mark's Church, estimates number of dead at 800
Police Inspector Brooks, directing the rescue work, estimates 1000

Bodies have been picked up as follows:

North Brother Island	128
Alexander Avenue Station	37
Tug Fidelity	88
Riker's Island	50
Oak Point	16
Total	**319**

black skirt, white dotted waist, black jacket, wedding ring.
Nos. 12, 13, 14, 15, 16, 17. Unidentified bodies of three infants and three children less than five years old.
No. 18—Woman about forty-five years old, 5 feet 4 inches, light hair, white waist, pepper and salt waist, button shoes.
No. 19—Woman fifty, 5 feet 1 inches, gray hair, black dress, earrings, a cross in amount in which dead women and children were laid out.
No. 20—Woman, forty, 5 feet 3 inches, black waist and light skirt, gold thumb.
No. 21 Woman, thirty-five, brown hair, very stout, black silk waist and black skirt, wedding ring.
No. 22 Woman, forty-five, check waist, gray skirt, black stockings and lace gaiter shoes.
No. 23. Woman, sixty, black jacket and skirt, black stockings, lace shoes.
No. 24 Woman, thirty-five; black satin waist, blue skirt, lace shoes. Later identified as Mrs. Selma Grimm.
No. 25 Woman, forty; check waist, black skirt, lace gaiters.
No. 26 Tall woman, black silk waist with beads, black skirt, black stockings and lace shoes.
No. 27. Woman, fifty, blue waist, brown jacket, green skirt, lace shoes.

CHILD IN PADDLE-BOX CALLED FOR "MAMMA"

Little One Was Lying Alive on Pile of Dead When Rescuers Extricated Bodies Tangled Among the Blades of Huge Wheel.

One of the rescuing fleet put in under the off shore paddle box of the Slocum and discovered several dead bodies of women and children lying on the blades of the paddle wheels.

In removing one of the bodies several other corpses dropped from their positions into the water.

On top of the pile of dead the rescuing party discovered a little girl crying and calling for "Mamma." She with the others had managed to reach the interior of the paddle box as a means of escape. She was the only one of the unfortunate lot that survived, the rest being burned to death.

Out of the peril from fire and water came four-year-old Lizzie Krieger without a smudge on her red gown, without a stain on her placid pretty face. She was taken to the Alexander avenue station, where she sat for two hours in a room in which dead women and children were laid out in more than long rows.

Her big brown eyes swept over the crowd, as it surged in and out seeking to identify perhaps the dead. To all inquirers she had but one reply:

"My mamma is all burned up. I saw her burn."

An Evening World reporter learned from her that she went to the excursion with her mother and her little brother. Her mother was caught in the flames and some one asked her and the boy. Where he is she doesn't know. She says that her home is in Fourteenth street, and it is probably in the vicinity of First avenue.

WORLD OPENS BUREAU TO AID SURVIVORS.

The World has opened an information bureau at No. 306 East Sixth street for the purpose of aiding survivors of the Slocum disaster in making known their safety and to help the relatives of the dead and missing to locate the bodies of their loved ones.

Requests will be kept at this bureau and all inquiries will be given careful attention. The telephone number is 2276 J Orchard and a reporter has been assigned to answer telephone calls of inquiry.

Bodies of Women and Children Still Coming Ashore at North Brother Island and Other Points Around Hell Gate --- Fire Caused by the Overturning of Pot of Grease in the Galley.

The big excursion steamboat Gen. Slocum burned and sank to-day off North Brother Island with 1,600 excursionists, 500 of them children from St. Mark's German Lutheran Church, in East Sixth street, aboard. The loss of life is estimated to be 1,000.

The following is the latest estimate made by Detective-Sergeant Kinsler and Police Inspector Brooks. Their computation is as follows:

Number on board	1,600
Dead bodies recovered	400
Injured in hospitals	300
Survivors accounted for	100
Missing	800

Fifty-three injured persons died on North Brother Island while the doctors were attending to them just after they had been carried from the boat to the shore.

When the Slocum went down, at 12.25 o'clock, two hours and twenty-five minutes after the fire was first discovered, it is estimated that there were nearly one hundred charred bodies on her decks. Every few minutes a body pops up from the wreck. The corpses of seven adults and one baby were towed from there to North Brother Island at 2 o'clock.

Just after the Slocum sank where she had drifted from North Brother Island the water was black with bodies. The tug Fidelity succeeded in picking up eighty-eight charred corpses before the swirling eddies in Hunt's Cove off Riker's Island carried them out into the Sound.

None of these eighty-eight bodies can ever be identified. Heads and legs are burned off. Not a shred of clothing is left on any one of them. The captain of the Fidelity says that he estimates that he left twenty bodies without trying to take them into the boat, because it would have been impossible to arrange them into any semblance of human remains.

WORST HARBOR HORROR.

In sudden paralyzing horror the tragedy has no parallel in the history of marine disasters in this harbor. Within half an hour a laughing, care-free crowd, bound for a day's outing in the country, was more than decimated by fire and water.

All the bodies in the Harlem Morgue, on North Brother Island, and at the station-houses, will be removed to the Manhattan Morgue at the foot of East Twenty-sixth street before midnight, and the Morgue will be kept open day and night.

Patrolmen Abel M. Van Tassel and Charles Kelt, who were detailed to the Gen. Slocum for the excursion, report to Commissioner McAdon that the fire started at 10.10 A. M. in the forecastle, when the boat was opposite One Hundred and Sixteenth street.

Coroner O'Gorman, who with a squad of police, made a detailed search of bodies for marks of identification, reports that about $180,000 worth of jewelry and money, or bank books representing money, were found upon the bodies.

FIRE STARTED IN POT OF GREASE.

According to Rev. Dr. Haas, the fire started in the galley from a pot of boiling fat when the boat was off the sunken meadows, opposite One Hundred and Thirty-fourth street. Instead of running its boat ashore at One Hundred and Thirty-fourth street, Capt. Van Schaick beached his off North Brother Island, a quarter of a mile away, and on this trip the flames

Ladies' Special.
Trimmed Hat nobuilt for $5.00, worth $5.00. Carriage rates and for at special closing our prices at Freuher & St. 59th and Grand Av., S.

The charred remains of the General Slocum.
[LOC, USZ62-138405]

Ten-year-old Walter Mueller barely avoided drowning. "After papa tied the life preserver around me I jumped into the water. The life preserver was of no use for it broke right off me, and I thought I was going to drown. I grabbed a man's neck and went under the water. When I came up again, I seized a woman by the hair and she scratched my face." Walter let go, and as he was sinking, a man in a boat grabbed him.

Tugs, ferries, fireboats, and police boats chased the *Slocum* and pulled people from the river. Mothers and fathers flung their daughters and sons into the water, hoping they would be rescued or at least be spared from burning to death. One tugboat captain braved the flames long enough for parents to drop their children onto the tug's deck. But to avoid catching fire, the tugboat had to pull away. The tug's captain said he would never forget the pleas and screams of the people he left behind.

Just before the *Slocum* reached North Brother Island, the bulkheads—a ship's walls—supporting the upper deck collapsed, spilling passengers into the flames below. The pilots tried to swing the boat around so its stern would be near shore. But the ship suddenly ran aground on submerged rocks. The bow, completely in flames, was just 20 feet from land, but the stern, where the surviving passengers were, was in deep water 270 feet from shore.

There was a last desperate attempt to save lives. Charles Swartz, Jr., an 18-year-old passenger, climbed into a boat and helped its owner rescue 22 people. "I went overboard whenever I could," he recalled, "and swam up to people and helped them in the boat." A Riverside Hospital switchboard operator swam out to the ship a dozen times, saving as many people as possible before she collapsed, exhausted.

Some passengers saved themselves in grisly ways. "I didn't have no life preserver at all," said ten-year-old Henry Ferneissen. "I went down twice and I swallowed a whole lot of water, but pretty soon I caught hold of a dead woman and then somebody grabbed me with a hook. If it hadn't been for that dead woman I'd been drowned sure."

One hour after embarking, the *General Slocum* was a smoldering ruin and most of its thirteen hundred passengers were dead. One survivor said, "To my dying day I'll never forget the scene. Around me were scores of bodies, most of them charred and burned."

Rescue workers fished hundreds of corpses from

A view of the paddle wheel and other debris on the burned-out steamship.
[LOC, USZ62-138402]

the water and pulled hundreds more from the wreckage. For several days afterward, people found corpses of men, women, and children washed up onshore or floating in the river. Some victims were never found.

```
[BERDOLT, Mrs. Gussie, 30 years, 1050 Prospect avenue]
BOEGER, Wilbur, 4 years, of 910 Putnam avenue.
BOEGER, Florence [A]., 4 years, of 910 Putnam avenue.
BOEGER, Mrs. William, 30 years, of 910 Putnam avenue.
Mrs. Susan L] [BREDA, Minnie, 29 years, of 150 North
Ninth street]
DIECKHOFF, Annie, 17 years, of 121 Fourth avenue.
DIECKHOFF, William, 8 years, of 4 Greene avenue.
DIECKHOFFF, ____, 20 years, of 121 Fourth avenue.
[DIECKHOFF, Marie, of 121 Fourth avenue]
[DIECKHOFF, Edward, of 121 Fourth avenue]
[DIECKHOFF, William H. of 121 Fourth avenue]
[EIMER, Kate, 45 years, of 84 Stockholm street]
[FLEGENHEIMER, Lena, of 608 Greene avenue]
GENDERT, William, of 538 Morgan avenue.
GERDES, Mrs. Margaret, 66 years, of 430 Kosciusko
street]
HEN[C]KEN, Charles, 17 [18] years, of 169, South Second
street.
HE[R]NBERG, George, 7 years, of 79 Calyer street.
HERNBERG, Arthur, 9 years, of 79 Calyer street
HOFFMAN, Mrs. Cecilia, 27 years, 336 New York avenue]
```

Partial list of the dead. [*Brooklyn Daily Eagle*, June 15, 1904]

No one knows exactly how many of *General Slocum*'s passengers died. The official estimate is 1,021. All of the *Slocum*'s crew survived.

A grand jury later indicted two government steamship inspectors, four Knickerbocker Steamship Company executives, and Captain Van Schaick. Only the captain was convicted of negligent homicide. The judge sentenced him to ten years in Sing Sing, an upstate New York prison. Meanwhile, federal officials made steamboat safety regulations more stringent and reformed the U.S. Steamboat Inspection Service.

The *General Slocum* tragedy is the worst peace-time maritime accident in American history. It was New York's deadliest disaster until the twenty-first century.

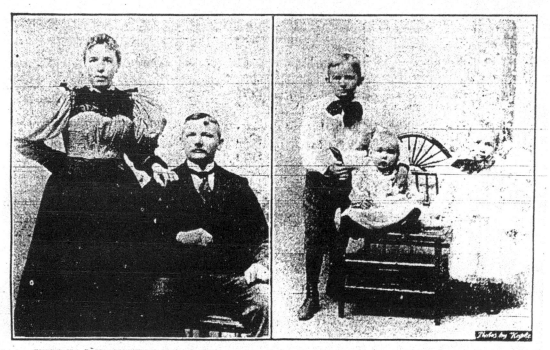

FIVE MEMBERS OF THE OELLRICH FAMILY OF BROOKLYN, LOST IN THE DISASTER.

The Father, William Oellrich, Survives, as Does the Boy Henry, Aged 11, Shown Standing in the Picture. The Mother, Annie, and the Two Little Ones in the Picture Are Missing, as Well as Two Other Children.

A family that lost five of its members to the fire. [*Brooklyn Daily Eagle,* June 15, 1904]

AMERICA'S LAST GREAT URBAN FIRE

SAN FRANCISCO, 1906

A half century after the 1849 California Gold Rush, San Francisco had become the Crown Jewel of the Pacific. It was the West Coast's largest city and, according to the 1900 census, the ninth-largest city in the United States. But three horrific days in April 1906 left San Francisco in ruins and its future in doubt.

At 5:12 A.M. on Wednesday, April 18, one of the strongest earthquakes ever recorded rumbled along the West Coast from Southern California north to Oregon and as far inland as Nevada. San Francisco was only two miles from the quake's epicenter. In just 48 seconds, the quake toppled hundreds of

buildings, felled utility poles, broke gas pipes, and ruptured storage tanks full of oil, gasoline, and kerosene. It also snapped most of the pipes supplying the city's water from outlying reservoirs.

The San Francisco Fire Department's seven hundred firefighters quickly turned out. At first, there were no fires visible, so they rescued people trapped in collapsed buildings. "At No. 313 Sixth St., the

[ABOVE] *Engine 15 several years before the 1906 fire.*
[LOC, HABS CAL,38-SANFRA,72--3]

[FACING PAGE] *Market Street, one of the city's main thoroughfares, before the fire.* [LOC, USZ62-98494]

Residents amid the earthquake's destruction,
watching the spreading fire. [LOC, G4085-0201]

place was completely wrecked and the bare foot of a child could be seen in a pile of debris," Captain C. J. Cullen of Engine Company No. 6 later wrote in his report. "We cut our way into the premises with axes and shortly afterwards rescued three little children and five adults." But soon the firefighters had to turn their attention to numerous fires, started by downed electrical wires and stoves in restaurants and homes, that had begun to flare up all across San Francisco.

South of Market Street, reporter James Hopper saw fire "swirling up the narrow way with a sound that was almost like a scream." At Third and Market, "the

[NEXT PAGE] *In just a few hours after the earthquake, San Francisco was in flames.* [LOC, USZ62-44926]

tallest skyscraper in the city was glowing like a phosphorescent worm," Hopper wrote, describing the 15-story Call Building, and "fire poured out of the thousand windows."

By evening, "the lower portion of Market Street, Chinatown, and Nob Hill was one seething furnace," observed another reporter. "Thousands of angry flames shot high into the sky, and the cracking timbers, the falling buildings, and the terrific roar of the fire sounded like a dozen cyclones."

Firefighters tapped every possible source of water, including the sewers. Resorting to colonial-era firefighting tactics, Engine Company No. 26 formed a bucket brigade from a well to a burning building. Other firemen tapped old underground

A piano company ablaze. [Pacific Earthquake Engineering Research
Center, University of California, Berkeley]

*Soldiers patrol the streets to prevent looting. The Call Building,
then the tallest building west of the Mississippi River,
looms in the background.* [LOC, USZ62-96789]

storage tanks, called cisterns, each holding between ten thousand and thirty thousand gallons of water. Sixty of them had been built a half century earlier, after a big fire in 1851 had leveled the young city.

At 17th and Howard streets, reported Captain Cullen, "there being considerable water in a large hole in the middle of the street owing to a broken main, with stones and sand we dammed the water that was running to waste and put our Engine to work after stretching hose as far as Capp St. near 16th St. Here we had a very hard fight as the wind was blowing the intense heat of the fire in our direction. Soon it became unbearable . . . but after fighting every inch of the ground we succeeded in getting it under control at 20th St."

One reliable water source was San Francisco Bay. "We laid a line from the Fire Boat to Broadway and Mason streets, a distance of fourteen blocks, taking about 4,000 feet of hose," reported Battalion Chief John McClusky. "The Fire Boat and three engines [were] all pumping on this single line, [and] with this one stream we worked vainly to prevent the fire from crossing the north side of Broadway."

The firefighters made one heroic stand after another. "Many of them dropped utterly exhausted at their post of duty, which was quickly taken up by one of their comrades," a writer observed. "They stood in the smoke of the roaring furnaces to fight the flames and cases are on record where police officers and volunteer firemen had to continually apply a stream of water on the regular firemen on duty in order to keep them from being burned or scorched."

The firefighters worked around the clock, snatching bits of sleep whenever they could. "When opportunity afforded," wrote Captain George F. Brown of Engine Company No. 2, his men "got an hour or two of rest in the doorways and in the streets alongside their apparatus, and the little they had to eat during these fifty hours of continuous service was given to them by kind-hearted people."

The crowds in the streets, said one observer, resembled war refugees: "thousands of families of women and little children dragged themselves from place to place in front of the flames, lying without shelter in vacant lots, exposed to fog and chilling rain."

The cold drizzle didn't slow the fire, so the firefighters created firebreaks. Dennis Sullivan, the city's chief fire engineer for 13 years, had been an expert on the use of explosives. But he and firefighter James O'Neil had been fatally injured in the earthquake. The men setting the explosives learned by trial and error. "It was an earth-racked night of terror," recalled one resident. "We watched the leaping

Firemen spraying a heavily damaged building. [LOC, USZ62-113371]

and hissing flames in the city below us, and heard the crashing of buildings. . . . By dynamiting buildings, the firemen hoped to check the conflagration. Much dynamite was used, many buildings blown to atoms, but all was in vain."

One explosion made the fire worse. The flames were nearly conquered, some observers believed, until the firefighters dynamited a building on Van Ness Avenue. The explosion spread the fire, which then destroyed another fifty blocks.

Hours later, firebreaks did work. "The great stand of the fire-fighters was made Thursday night on Van

Ness Avenue," wrote novelist Jack London, who came from his home across the bay to see the fire. "Had they failed here, the comparatively few remaining houses of the city would have been swept. Here were the magnificent residences of the second generation of San Francisco nabobs, and these, in a solid zone, were dynamited down across the path of the fire. Here and there the flames leaped the zone, but these fires were beaten out, principally by the use of wet blankets and rugs."

In three days, the fire destroyed 28,188 buildings on 490 city blocks. It covered 2,600 acres, 600 acres more than the Great Chicago Fire. The disaster left half of the city's 410,000 residents homeless. "Not in history has a modern imperial city been so completely destroyed," wrote London. "San Francisco is gone."

Civic leaders tried to downplay the tragedy, historians believe, because they didn't want people to think San Francisco was an unsafe place to live or work. They reported a death toll of 376 people. Years later, researchers discovered over three thousand had died in the earthquake and fire.

Jack London, an author best known for his novel The Call of the Wild, *wrote a firsthand account of the fire.*
[LOC, G399-0200]

A photograph of Market Street that appears to have been taken from an overhead balloon. [LOC, USZ62-49317]

Devastation. [LOC, USZ62-47147]

San Francisco quickly rebuilt homes and businesses. Workmen repaired the broken pipes and 54 of the old cisterns. Then they added 85 cisterns, each holding 75,000 gallons of water. In 1954, the city constructed Summit Reservoir, which holds fourteen million gallons of water at Twin Peaks, the city's second-highest point. If that runs out, two pumping stations can refill the reservoir by drawing water from the bay. Even with these precautions, San Francisco never quite regained all of its luster. By 1920, Los Angeles had become the West Coast's largest city.

The San Francisco fire was America's last "great" city fire. More effective firefighting equipment, better-trained firefighters, reliable water supplies, strong fire codes, and modern building materials have all made large-scale fires less likely.

A weary-looking man trudging up one of San Francisco's steep hills. [LOC, USZ62-47591]

DEADLY WORKPLACE FIRE

NEW YORK, 1911

New York City fire chief Edward F. Croker knew that the city's factories would be much safer if owners installed fire walls, fire doors, fire stairs, and automatic sprinklers, as New England's factories had done in the nineteenth century. Not wanting to spend money on these safety features, the factory owners joined together to stop the city from enacting new safety regulations. It took a tragedy to change that.

The Triangle Waist Company in Manhattan's Greenwich Village made women's shirtwaists, which is what blouses were called in 1911. The company occupied the top three floors of the Asch Building, a ten-story brick structure on the corner of Greene

Street and Washington Place. The building had large windows and open floors about the size of two side-by-side basketball courts. On the eighth and ninth floors, hundreds of young women operated sewing machines at long wooden tables.

On the tenth floor, workers ironed and prepared finished blouses for shipping. The company's owners, Max Blanck and Isaac Harris, who were dubbed the "Shirtwaist Kings" because their company was the garment's largest manufacturer, also had offices on that floor.

The Shirtwaist Kings, in the middle, surrounded by their workers. [Kheel Center, Cornell University]

Two years earlier, the company had gained national notoriety because of the "Uprising of 20,000." Because of low wages and unsafe working conditions, Triangle employees walked off the job and went on strike. The protest spread to other garment factories. After four months, most manufacturers agreed to increase wages and make their factories safer, but not Max Blanck and Isaac Harris. Since jobs were scarce for new immigrants, the Shirtwaist Kings had no trouble finding new workers.

Clara Lemlich, one of the leaders of the Uprising of 20,000.
[Kheel Center, Cornell University]

On Saturday, March 25, about five hundred people were working at the Triangle Waist Company. While there were some men, most of the workers were Italian, Russian, or German women in their teens and twenties. Some worked as cutters, snipping the fabric into patterns, while others sewed the patterns together.

A couple of minutes before the 4:45 quitting time, workers were eyeing the door. It was payday and the end of their six-day workweek. Leaving work was often slow because employees had to file past the partition between the sewing room and the elevators so a foreman could check handbags to make sure no one was stealing. And each of the two elevators held only 12 people.

Just as the workers on the eighth floor turned off

A garment factory similar to the Triangle Waist Company.
[Kheel Center, Cornell University]

their sewing machines for the day, Eva Harris ran across the room, shouting, "Fire. There is a fire, Mr. Bernstein." This wasn't the first time Samuel Bernstein, the foreman, had heard a worker yell "Fire." Sometimes an electrical spark or a male cutter careless with a cigarette started a fire. That's why the foreman kept buckets of water handy.

Bernstein saw smoke and flames near Isidore Abramowitz's cutting table on the Greene Street side of the building. The foreman and the cutter threw water on the fire but weren't able to put it out. Other men grabbed a hose connected to a pipe from the rooftop water tank, but for some reason, there was no water.

Cotton, which burns more quickly than paper, was everywhere—under sewing machines, stacked on tables, and hanging from wires above the seamstresses. As flames raced through the room, Bernstein shouted, "Get out of here as fast as you can." About 180 people worked on that floor. They crowded into the aisles between the tables and pushed one another toward the stairwells and elevators.

The building had a stairwell on the Greene Street side and one on the Washington Placc side. City construction codes required three stairwells, but inspectors had allowed the builder to substitute an 18-inch-wide metal fire escape in the air shaft behind the Asch Building.

A man and several women climbed onto the fire escapc. They didn't know it ended above a skylight, with no way out of the air shaft. But they didn't like the flimsy metal fire escape, so they broke a sixth-floor window and climbed through.

Other workers on the eighth floor squeezed onto elevators or hurried down the Greene Street stairwell. At the door to the Washington Place stairs, there was a near fatal delay. That stairwell door opened inward, but the pushing and shoving crowd accidentally pinned several workers against the door, so it couldn't open. Louis Brown, a machinist, pushed people out of the way and flung the door open.

Before fleeing, a bookkeeper called the switchboard operator on the tenth floor to warn the sixty or so workers there. Without thinking of connecting the call to the ninth floor, where over two hundred people worked, the operator ran to tell her bosses.

Hearing shouts, Isaac Harris came out of his office. Looking through the air shaft windows, he saw smoke and flames. The heat suddenly shattered the glass and ignited stacks of blouses. Harris yelled for everyone to go up the Greene Street stairwell, the only one leading to the roof. The hot, smoke-filled stairwell, survivors later said, made them feel like they were running straight into the fire.

By then, the flames had reached the ninth floor. Workers there couldn't go down the Greene Street stairs because of the eighth-floor fire. In their panic, most probably didn't think about going up. Others tried the stairs across the room.

"I ran to the Washington Place door," said 16-year-old Ethel Monick, "but found it locked. I tried and tried to open it." Managers sometimes locked the doors to keep employees from sneaking out early. As Monick looked for another way to escape, the nearby elevator opened and the people rushing into the car swept her along with them.

No one remembered how often the elevators returned to the ninth floor that afternoon. As the doors were closing on his last trip, elevator operator Joseph Zito said, "all I could see was a crowd of girls and men with great flames and smoke right behind them."

Some workers who couldn't squeeze into an elevator jumped onto the descending car's roof or tried to slide down its cables. "I reached out, grabbed the cables, wrapped my legs around them and started to slide down," recalled Samuel Levine, a ninth-floor sewing machine operator. "I can remember getting to the sixth floor. While on my way down, as slow as I could let myself drop, the bodies of six girls went past me. One of them struck me and I fell to the top of the elevator. I fell on the dead body of a girl." Firefighters later found 19 bodies atop the two elevators.

The Asch Building was one of the new "fireproof" buildings. [Kheel Center, Cornell University]

The flimsy fire escape that killed more people than it saved. [Kheel Center, Cornell University]

Other workers on the ninth floor tried the only way left, the fire escape. Some climbed down, but others climbed up toward the roof, where college students who had been attending classes in the adjoining building were rescuing Blanck and Harris and their employees. Few people on the fire escape reached safety. Their weight made the metal buckle and they plunged to their deaths.

The New York Fire Department received the alarm at 4:45. Three minutes later, horses pulling a steam fire engine galloped down Greene Street. Seven more engines

FDNY firefighters on their way to the fire. [LOC, USZ62-34985]

and hook and ladder companies soon followed. The firefighters saw flames and smoke pouring from the top three floors of the Asch Building and people standing in the ninth-floor windows. The firefighters quickly put up their tallest ladder, but it reached only to the sixth floor.

As fire filled the entire ninth floor, a man stepped out of a window and fell one hundred feet to the sidewalk. Then another man helped four women onto a window ledge and watched them step off before he followed.

Louis Waldman, a witness to the scene, said, "Horrified and helpless, the crowds—I among

One of the burned-out floors. [Kheel Center, Cornell University]

them—looked up at the burning building, saw girl after girl appear at the reddened windows, pause for a terrified moment, and then leap to the pavement below. . . . This went on for what seemed a ghastly eternity. Occasionally a girl who had hesitated too long was licked by pursuing flames and, screaming with clothing and hair ablaze, plunged like a living

Firefighters spraying the building. [Kheel Center, Cornell University]

Mourners line the streets during a funeral procession for victims of the Triangle fire, April 5, 1911. [Kheel Center, Cornell University]

torch to the street." About fifty people jumped or fell to their deaths.

In only 12 minutes, the fire had raced through three floors. By the time the firefighters extinguished it, 146 people had died, some as young as 15.

Weeks later, the Shirtwaist Kings were on trial for criminal negligence, but their lawyer won an acquittal. Their insurance company paid each victim's family about $75. A New York State commission investigated safety problems in the state's industries, which led to increased fire-safety awareness and to new laws protecting workers.

The Triangle Shirtwaist tragedy sparked many labor protests. [Kheel Center, Cornell University]

Edward F. Croker, who had joined the Fire Department of New York at age 18 and was chief by age 33, resigned after the Triangle Shirtwaist fire to start a fire-prevention company. Chief Croker could be called "the father of the fire drill," because he was among the first to conduct fire drills in factories and offices. He taught employees to stay calm and orderly while quickly leaving by designated exits. Fire drills, Chief Croker believed, were one of the best ways to save lives.

The man tipping his hat is Fire Chief Edward Croker.
[New York City Fire Museum]

*A political cartoon critical of New York's building code
inspectors.* [Kheel Center, Cornell University]

NIGHTCLUB TRAGEDY

BOSTON, 1942

At 10:15 P.M. on November 28, 1942, Engine Company No. 35 answered an alarm for a car fire in Boston's downtown entertainment district. By 10:20, the four firefighters had extinguished the fire and were returning to the engine house, when they saw smoke pouring from the Cocoanut Grove.

This popular nightclub occupied a yellow stucco building with entrances on Shawmut and Piedmont streets. That first Saturday after Thanksgiving, some one thousand people, nearly double its legal capacity, filled the Cocoanut Grove. More had lined up outside, hoping to get in.

"It was so crowded that you had to turn sideways

to get through the tables in the dining room," said Hewson Gray, who was having dinner with his wife and friends. Many sailors and soldiers were there. Other people in the club had attended that afternoon's football game between fierce rivals Boston College and Holy Cross.

The nightclub had several rooms decorated in a tropical theme, with colorful fabric covering the ceiling and artificial seven-foot-tall palm trees made of bamboo and satin. In the basement was the Melody Lounge, where Goody Goodelle played the piano while couples snuggled at tables in the dark shadows and customers at the bar stood four-deep. Upstairs were two more bars, a dance floor, and a dining room full of closely spaced tables draped in white linen. That evening, the house band, Mickey Alpert and His Orchestra, started their performance with the national anthem.

At about 10:15 in the Melody Lounge, 16-year-old bar boy Stanley Tomaszewski struck a match so that he could see to replace a lightbulb someone had unscrewed, perhaps to have more privacy with his date. The match stayed lit just for a moment, but long enough to ignite a fake palm tree. Waiters and bartenders tried to douse the flames with water and then with a fire extinguisher, but the fire spread too quickly.

"There was a flash. Fire ran right across the ceiling," head bartender John Bradley said. As flames ignited the sky blue satin cloth ceiling, some two hundred customers stared for a second in disbelief. Then, knocking over tables and chairs, they rushed to the main stairs, leading up to the club's front entrance on Piedmont Street. Bradley led a group through the kitchen, which was next to the Melody Lounge, and up the stairs to a rear door leading to an alley. It was locked.

The Cocoanut Grove had several exits. But the managers didn't want people skipping out without paying their tabs. They locked or concealed all the doors except the main one to Piedmont Street and the one through the bar to Shawmut Street.

When the ceiling ignited in the Melody Lounge, Daniel Weiss, a Boston University medical student working behind the bar, grabbed a wet towel to cover his face, dropped to the floor, and took only shallow breaths to avoid inhaling too much smoke. "The closer I was to the floor, the easier it was to breathe," Weiss said later. Then, holding his breath, he scrambled across the bar and stumbled over lifeless people to get to the kitchen. He was surprised to find some two dozen men and women there, all wondering where to go.

Unaware the fire had already spread to the main

floor, Weiss started up the kitchen stairs to the dining room, but the heat drove him back. Next, he tried another stairway. Weiss told the people in the kitchen to follow him, but they thought it was too dangerous. After groping his way up the dark stairs, Weiss found John Bradley and several other men throwing their weight against the alley door. Suddenly, a firefighter yelled for everyone to step back. Then a fire ax splintered the door, letting in a rush of cold air.

Journalist Martin Sheridan recalled the scene in the dining room: "We had just been served an oyster cocktail when, above the babble someone at the end of our table screamed, 'Fire!' Then I heard the loud crackling of flames consuming the tropical

Toxic smoke hampered the rescue. [Boston Public Library]

decorations." Drawn by abundant oxygen on the spacious main floor, the fire had burst up the stairwell.

The diners ran to the Piedmont Street exit, which was a revolving door. People desperately pushed in opposite directions on the revolving door, and no one could get out. They struggled against the glass as onlookers on the street watched helplessly.

The headwaiter, Frank Balzarini, shouted for customers to follow him through a concealed dining room door to the street. Some thirty to forty people escaped before the lights went out and thick toxic smoke filled the room. Balzarini fought his way back inside, no doubt trying to help others. He died in the fire.

Firefighter George "Red" Graney of Engine Company No. 35 was connecting a hose to a hydrant on Shawmut Street when he saw his three partners run to help a burning man who had stumbled out of the Cocoanut Grove. Behind the man, the crush of people jammed against the door, which swung inward and couldn't be opened. The firefighters struggled to force it open. "It was incredible," Graney recalled. "I couldn't go forward or to the right because of the bodies. I couldn't even get in with the hose."

He finally managed to push partway in and turn

Soldiers and sailors helped remove the victims. [Boston Public Library]

on his high-pressure hose. On the roof, firefighters chopped holes so that heat, smoke, and toxic gases could escape and be less of a danger to rescue workers and survivors inside.

After the fire was out, officials found some two

An injured fireman being helped to an ambulance. [Boston Public Library]

hundred bodies piled chest-high behind the revolving door. In the hallway to the stairs down to the Melody Lounge, one investigator said, it looked as though the victims had clawed and fought one another while trying to escape. One firefighter who had been pulling people to safety had scratches on his legs from people desperately clutching at him.

Graney described the dining room on the main floor: "The tables weren't all burnt and in some places people, though dead, were only singed, still at their chairs and drooped over their tables. Yet elsewhere other bodies were so badly burned you couldn't tell the men from the women."

Firefighter John Collins said the damage in the Melody Lounge was mostly along the ceiling. "Of all the vivid impressions made upon me that evening," he added, "perhaps the most unforgettable was . . . a very pretty girl. She was sitting with her eyes open and her hand on a cocktail glass, as if waiting for someone. As I first looked at her I wondered why she was just sitting there, thinking she was okay. But, of course, she was dead."

Rescue workers rushed the injured to hospitals and carried the dead across the street to a garage

[NEXT PAGE] *One of the Cocoanut Grove bars.*
[Boston Public Library]

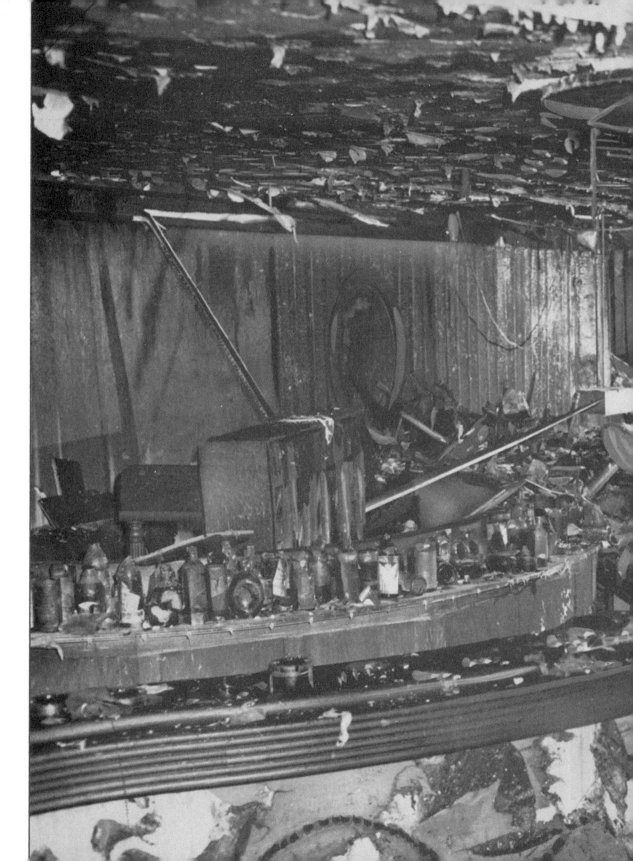

being used as a temporary morgue. "At the time we had no idea how many were killed," Graney said, "and we guessed that maybe 200 people had been lost."

Many of the victims didn't burn to death; they died from inhaling smoke and toxic gas from chemicals in the furniture and leather-covered walls. To protect themselves from smoke and lethal gases, some survivors, like Daniel Weiss, had the presence of mind to cover their noses and mouths with wet towels or clothing. One man used a napkin he had urinated on.

The fire killed 492 people. That's more than in all of Boston's great fires of the eighteenth and nineteenth

The charred nightclub a day after the fire. [Boston Public Library]

Stacks of coffins for the victims. [Boston Public Library]

centuries combined. The Cocoanut Grove fire is the deadliest nightclub fire in U.S. history.

Over the following months, Boston officials strengthened building- and fire-safety codes. New regulations banned flammable decorations in restaurants and other public establishments. And they required lighted exit signs, doors that open outward, and regular doors flanking revolving doors.

Research doctors at Boston's academic hospitals learned a great deal about treating burns as well as trauma and grief while attending to the Cocoanut Grove victims. Little was known about trauma and the grieving process until Dr. Erich Lindemann, a Harvard University psychiatrist, interviewed survivors of the fire and relatives of the deceased for the first formal study of grief. That study helped develop new ways of coping with bereavement. Researchers also discovered that blood-plasma transfusions helped patients in severe shock. And they credited penicillin, a new drug being tested, for helping third-degree-burn victims recover.

A victim being treated at a Boston hospital. [Boston Public Library]

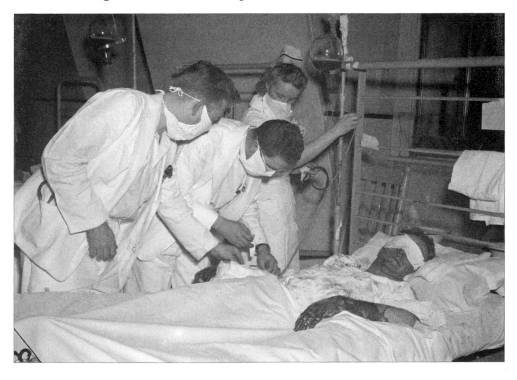

9/11
FIRE IN THE SKY

 NEW YORK, 2001

At 8:46 A.M. on Tuesday, September 11, 2001, Battalion Chief Joseph Pfeifer and the New York City firefighters of Engine Company No. 7 were investigating a gas leak in lower Manhattan when they heard an airliner roar overhead. They saw the blue-and-white markings of an American Airlines passenger jet just before it crashed into the upper floors of the North Tower, one of the twin skyscrapers at the World Trade Center.

Chief Pfeifer jumped into the department's red SUV and, lights flashing and Klaxon blaring, sped fifteen blocks down Church Street to the Trade

Center. On the way, he called in first, second, and third alarms, summoning nineteen fire trucks.

On the wide Trade Center plaza, Pfeifer had to dodge falling concrete, steel, glass, and pieces of the airliner. Jet fuel inside the North Tower had flooded the elevator shaft, causing a fiery explosion on the ground floor that blew elevator doors open, cracked the marble-tiled walls, and shattered the thick glass wrapped around the cavernous lobby. Several people were badly burned.

Within five minutes of Chief Pfeifer's call, the first engine companies arrived. Lieutenant Kevin Pfeifer, the chief's younger brother by three years, was with Engine Company No. 33. The chief sent his brother and five other firefighters up the stairs to report on conditions on the higher floors.

Back in 1968, construction on the $1.5 billion World Trade Center began, and the two 110-story towers were finished by 1972. At that time, the two buildings, popularly known as the Twin Towers, were the world's tallest structures. They were slightly higher

The Twin Towers before September 11, 2001. [LOC-DIG--15556]

than thirteen hundred feet. That's a quarter of a mile straight up.

Below street level was a six-story basement with more space than the entire Empire State Building. The Mall at the World Trade Center—with some 55 stores and restaurants, such as the Gap, Borders bookstore, and Sbarro—occupied the concourse level where tens of thousands of people daily flowed from the World Trade Center's two subway stations.

The World Trade Center rented offices to brokerage firms, advertising agencies, insurance companies, banks, and government agencies like the FBI and CIA. A sculptor had a studio on the North Tower's 92nd floor. On weekdays, about forty thousand people worked in the Trade Center and thousands more visited. At the beginning of that Tuesday's workday, about sixteen thousand people were in the complex.

The airliner, its wings tilted, hit the North Tower, traveling at 450 miles per hour. The long wings sliced through the 93rd to 99th floors. The impact caused the tower to sway and the earth to tremble, registering on seismographs 22 miles away. The explosion of eleven thousand gallons of jet fuel created

A United Airlines passenger jet crashes into the South Tower of the World Trade Center. [AP Photo/Carmen Taylor]

The airliner's jet fuel exploded when it hit the South Tower. [AP Photo/Carmen Taylor]

a fireball so hot that people inside the South Tower, two hundred feet away, felt the heat. The crash knocked out the North Tower's public-address system, the overhead sprinklers, and most of the 99 elevators, stranding passengers inside the cars.

In the first ten minutes after the crash, New York's 911 system received some three thousand calls. Many were from people trapped above the 99th floor. They said smoke was filling their offices and they wanted to know what they should do. The three stairwells in the middle of thc building—the only way down when the elevators didn't work—were blocked with rubble or filled with smoke and flames. The emergency operators could offer only standard advice: Stay low to avoid breathing smoke and wait for emergency personnel.

The New York City Police Department dispatched some one thousand officers to lower Manhattan. Two NYPD helicopters hovered near the towers to report on conditions on the upper floors. Police closed the nearby West Side Highway and other major arteries to all traffic except emergency vehicles.

FDNY dispatchers sent 21 engine companies and 11 ladder companies manned by a total of two hundred firefighters. And hundreds of off-duty firefighters rushed downtown to help. The department's top brass set up a command center, which is called a staging area, across the street from the North Tower, while mid-level commanders gave orders from the lobby.

The commanders knew, as one of them later explained, that a "large volume of fire on the upper floors" would be impossible to put out. And knowing several floors might collapse, "we determined, very early on, that this was going to be strictly a rescue mission. We were going to vacate the building, get everybody out, and then we were going to get out."

Division Chief Peter Hayden said, "We had a very strong sense we would lose firefighters and that we were in deep trouble."

People trapped above the North Tower's 99th floor sent e-mails or made cell phone calls to wives and husbands, mothers and fathers, children and friends.

At street level near the World Trade Center. [LOC-DIG-ppmsca-02121-0064]

Two *New York Times* reporters collected e-mails and messages left on answering machines and interviewed relatives of victims to piece together the scene inside the tower.

Pete Alderman, who was attending a meeting in the famous Windows on the World restaurant on the 106th floor, exchanged e-mails with his sister Jane.

"I'm SCARED," he wrote, "THERE IS A lot OF SMOKE."

"can you get out of there?" she asked.

"No we are stuck."

Down on the North Tower's 88th floor, Frank De Martini was having coffee in his office with his wife, Nicole, who worked in the South Tower. De Martini was the construction manager in charge of renovations at the World Trade Center. When the airliner struck, De Martini told his wife and his employees, about thirty people, to start down the one passable stairwell below the 93rd floor. De Martini and three other men went from office to office on the 88th floor, making sure no one was left behind.

When the men started down the stairs, they heard banging on the stairwell door from the floor above. Grabbing hard hats, a flashlight, and a crowbar, they went up to the 89th floor. The stairwell door was jammed. De Martini used the crowbar to break through the drywall around the frame and dislodge the door. As people hurried down the stairs, the four men searched the floor for others who were trapped or didn't know that one stairwell offered an escape.

Office workers in the South Tower heard the horrific crash but didn't know what had happened. On the upper floors, workers on the tower's northern side crowded around the tall, narrow windows and saw thick black smoke flowing from gashes in the North Tower.

Some of these people had been at the Trade Center in 1993, when terrorists tried to topple the North Tower by detonating a thirteen-hundred-pound truck bomb in the underground garage. It wrecked the huge basement, killed six people, and injured one thousand. Evacuating both towers took hours.

Because of that experience eight years earlier, many workers in the South Tower immediately headed for the elevators. When the first people leaving got to the lobby, the security guard asked, "Where are you guys going? . . . All is well here. You can go back to your office. This building is secure." Some left, while most went back up.

Just before 9:00 A.M., an announcement over the public-address system repeated the guard's assurances: An incident had occurred in the North Tower, but the South Tower was safe. Everyone should stay in their offices.

Then the fire chiefs decided the North Tower fire endangered the whole complex, so the South Tower should be evacuated. Before that decision could be announced over the public-address system, a United Airlines plane going 540 miles an hour crashed into the South Tower between floors 77 and 85.

At his station uptown on 100th Street, Commander Richard Picciotto, the 50-year-old chief of Battalion 11, was watching television news and saw the second plane hit. Picciotto had been among the hundreds of firefighters who had helped evacuate the Trade Center after the 1993 bombing. Thinking his experience would be helpful, he rushed downtown.

Amid wailing sirens and flashing lights, "dodging bodies and glass and falling office equipment," Chief Picciotto ran to the North Tower's lobby. Reminiscent of the Triangle Shirtwaist fire nearly one hundred years earlier, people from the upper floors were jumping to avoid burning to death. He later learned that Danny Suhr, the first firefighter killed that day, had been hit by a falling body. Then FDNY chaplain Mychal Judge was killed by falling debris as he gave Suhr the Catholic Church's last rites.

In the North Tower's lobby Deputy Chief Pete Hayden told Picciotto to look for civilians on the 21st and 25th floors. The chief picked half a dozen men

Firefighters searching for survivors. [LOC-DIG-ppmsca-02121-0136]

from Brooklyn's Company No. 110 to follow him. Those men carried about one hundred pounds of gear, including cylinders of compressed air, axes, hooks, rabbit tools (hydraulic tools for forcing open doors), 150 feet of nylon rope, Halligans (a type of crowbar), and a length of hose called a roll-up. And their clothing—turnout coat, pants, boots, and helmet—weighed another thirty pounds.

With only a communications radio, flashlight, bullhorn, mask, and an air cylinder on his back, Picciotto sprinted ahead. After making sure no civilians were on either floor, he kept going up and checking floors. On the 35th, he saw three dozen firefighters waiting for orders. As the highest-ranking officer there, Picciotto had to decide what they should do. He knew that after three hours, a fire can bend a skyscraper's steel frame and cause the building to collapse.

A few minutes before 10:00 A.M. policemen in the two helicopters saw the South Tower leaning. They radioed NYPD commanders who immediately ordered all policemen out of that tower. Just 56 minutes after being struck, the burning tower crumbled.

As dust and rubble from the collapsed building filled the North Tower's lobby, the FDNY commanders ducked behind an escalator and got on their radios. "All units, tower 1, evacuate the building."

But the men up in the tower carried old radios that didn't work well, if at all, in skyscrapers. Few heard the order. And police and FDNY radios didn't share a frequency, nor did the two departments coordinate communications.

On the North Tower's 35th floor, Chief Picciotto heard "a bone-chilling roar and rumble." What was it? An explosion? Another airliner crashing? The chief got on his radio. "We just had a huge noise in the building. Does anybody know what happened?" There was no response for several seconds. Then a voice over the radio said just four words: "The Tower came down." Picciotto had to decide what to do. If one tower had collapsed, the other could, too.

For Picciotto, as for most firefighters, *retreat* wasn't normally in his vocabulary. But it had been over an hour since the first plane struck, the chief reasoned, so the floors below where it had hit should be clear of civilians. That settled it.

"Get out!" he yelled. "Let's start moving! Drop your masks! Drop your tools! Drop everything!" The firefighters trotted down stairwell C, but the pace soon slowed as other evacuating rescue workers filled the narrow stairwell.

[NEXT PAGE] *Destruction everywhere.*
[LOC-DIG-ppmsca-02121-0122]

On his way down, Picciotto checked each floor for civilians. On the 12th floor, he saw sixty people waiting for something—it wasn't clear what. He ordered them to evacuate immediately. "And as they moved toward me, I thought I was seeing things," he recalled. "There were people in wheelchairs, people on crutches, people moving with the aid of walkers and canes, people hardly moving at all." About half of them weren't impaired. They were helping friends and coworkers who were. The chief, over their protests, told the able-bodied to evacuate while firefighters helped the others.

One person needing help was a 59-year-old bookkeeper named Josephine Harris, who had already walked down 61 flights of stairs. Harris's legs were swollen and her breathing was labored. Picciotto followed as she took one step and then rested a couple of seconds before taking another.

After five floors, Chief Picciotto heard a noise he described as "earsplitting, bone-chilling, knee-trembling . . . every-damn-body-part-shaking, all multiplied out by about a million" and the wind was "just shy of gale force." As chunks of concrete crashed around him, in a fight-or-flight reaction he bounded down the stairs two at a time. At about the sixth floor, something hit the chief. "Whatever it was had whacked me pretty good, and I was down and thinking that would be it." Then everything went black.

The North Tower, after burning 102 minutes, had collapsed at 10:28 A.M.

Even though his mind seemed aware, Picciotto at first couldn't hear or feel. The chief soon realized he wasn't dead, just buried alive under a mountain of concrete. He shouted for the others. Out of the dark came responses from 14 men and Harris.

Exhausted firefighters. [LOC-DIG-ppmsca-02121-0230]

Several hours later, Picciotto and his men had managed to climb up to a door leading to a section of floor missing its outer wall. They used their ropes to rappel down the ten-story mountain of debris. It took several hours to rescue Harris, who was bruised but okay. Only four other people in the rubble were found alive.

Searchers later uncovered Kevin Pfeifer's body. Somewhere under the pile of smoldering concrete

A firefighter overcome by emotion. [LOC-DIG-ppmsca-02159]

and steel was Pete Alderman, one of the 160 people that morning in the Windows on the World restaurant. Also beneath the debris were De Martini and his three colleagues. Some sixty to seventy survivors remembered the men guiding them to the one passable stairwell to safety.

Rescue workers and survivors soon learned what had caused the tragedy. Terrorists had hijacked four airliners, two from Boston, one from Newark, and one from Dulles Airport, near Washington, D.C. All four planes were bound for California and had full fuel tanks. A half hour after the second plane hit the World Trade Center, terrorists crashed the airliner from Dulles into the Pentagon, located across the Potomac River from the nation's capital, and killed 125 people.

The fourth airliner, with 44 passengers and a crew of 7, didn't hit its target, believed to be the White House or the Capitol. The passengers attacked the hijackers, and the plane crashed near Shanksville, Pennsylvania.

At the World Trade Center, according to the office of the chief medical examiner of New York, 2,749 people died. They included 147 passengers and crew on the two airplanes, an estimated 600 people on the floors the airliners hit, and an estimated 1,500 people above those floors. A total of 412 rescue workers died, including 8 medics, 23 city police, 37 transit police, and 343 firefighters. More firefighters died that day than in the entire history of the FDNY.

The massive pile of rubble from the Twin Towers, which burned for three more months before it was finally extinguished, was cleared away the following year. Construction of the new World Trade Center began in 2006. The complex includes the National September 11 Memorial and Museum. The memorial, two large reflecting pools where the Twin Towers once stood, is called Reflecting Absence.

The new World Trade Center and the water memorial.
[National September 11 Memorial and Museum]

WILDFIRE

SAN DIEGO COUNTY, 2007

"The whole county is on fire," said Battalion Chief Ray Chaney, a U.S. Forest Service firefighter in San Diego County, where one of California's worst wildfires began Sunday morning, October 21, 2007.

For weeks, Southern California had been on red-flag alert because of dangerous fire conditions. Daily temperatures were in the nineties and the region was having a record-breaking drought. Plus, the annual Santa Ana winds, which usually start in November and last through January, were early. They swept in from the Mojave Desert on the Arizona and California border at thirty to forty miles per hour.

Firefighters name wild-fires after the place where they begin. This one started at Witch Creek in northeast San Diego County, so they called it the Witch Creek Fire or simply the Witch Fire. Firefighters believed the blaze started when sparks from electrical arcs along power lines ignited dry brush. These volts of electricity flash through the air from one conductor—power lines, in this case—to another.

Feeding on willow trees, cottonwoods, and low tangled brush called chaparral, the Witch Fire grew quickly. Strong winds sent it racing toward Ramona, a city of palm trees, horses, million-dollar homes, and 35,000 residents.

Fire on Mount San Miguel, about 17 miles east of San Diego.
[*San Diego Times Union*]

The Forest Service workers at Ramona Airport included Air Attack Base Manager Deborah Lutz. This soft-spoken 50-year-old with a long blond ponytail was in charge of four airplane tankers and three spotter planes. The tankers, when not grounded by high winds or thick smoke, flew over fires, dropping water and strawberry-colored fire-retardant chemicals. The strawberry color helped pilots see where they had previously dropped retardant. The small spotter planes searched for new fires and radioed their location to the airport.

Lutz and her crew focused their efforts on Mount Woodson, where a blaze threatened a communications tower used by the FBI, San Diego County sheriff, California Highway Patrol, and county emergency services. She also had more immediate problems.

A fire in the brush beside the runway, probably started by a firebrand, threatened to close the airport. No firefighters were immediately available, but they soon arrived and quickly extinguished the burning brush. Several miles away, the Witch Fire had burned the power line to Ramona's main water pump. Fortunately, the airport had an emergency pump powered by a gasoline generator.

In Ramona, the Witch Fire destroyed hundreds of homes and buildings. Then the winds drove it

Fire threatened thousands of homes near Irvine, California.
[AP Photo/Chris Carlson]

through 14 miles of canyons and hills to Poway, a city of fifty thousand people, located just 23 miles northeast of San Diego. The fire, Poway Fire Division Chief Kevin Kitch said, "was fast, hard, furious. It was push, push, push, push."

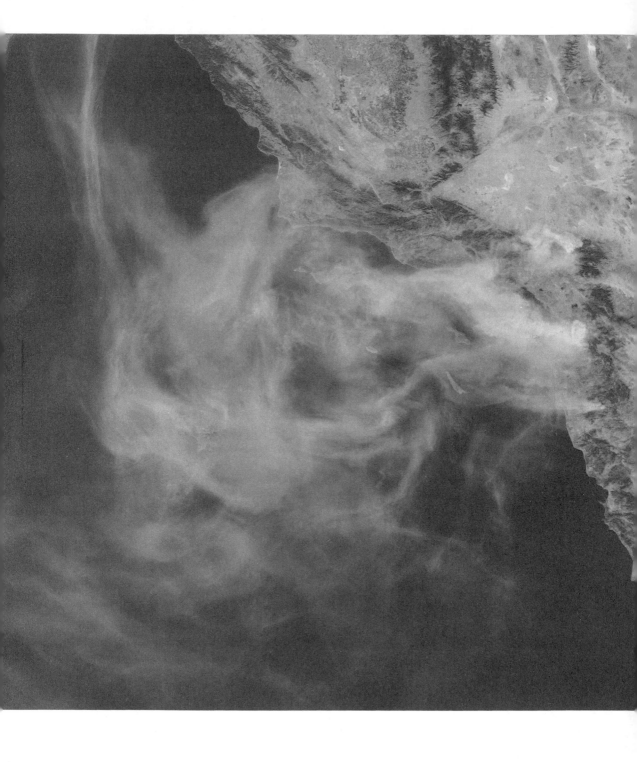

To make things worse, a second fire started forty miles away on the Harris Ranch, near the Mexican border in southern San Diego County. And the following day, over a dozen other fires broke out around the county. An arsonist started one, a 10-year-old boy playing with matches a second, and downed power lines caused others.

"The perimeter of the fire is huge," said Battalion Chief Chaney. "You're looking at an entire pillar of fire from the Mexican border to the Palomars," a mountain range in northern San Diego County.

Governor Arnold Schwarzenegger issued a state of emergency and President George W. Bush declared Southern California a national disaster area. To help fight the fire, the governor called out fifteen hundred National Guardsmen. Officials also brought in three thousand inmates who were serving prison sentences for nonviolent crimes. The Naval Air Station North Island in San Diego sent MH-60 Seahawk helicopters equipped with huge buckets for carrying water from Lake Ramona to drop on the fire.

The Witch Fire could easily be seen from space. [NASA]

Modern firefighters use helicopters and airplanes to battle wildfires. This helicopter and crew is from the Navy Reserves Sea Combat Squadron in San Diego. [U.S. Northern Command Public Affairs]

Firefighters from neighboring Arizona and Nevada rushed to San Diego County. And forty firefighters, called *bomberos* in Spanish, came from Tijuana, Mexico. Firefighters feel a strong bond for one another. "There isn't a difference between the firefighters here or on that side of the border," said 30-year-old *bombero* Jorge Villegas. "We're all *hermanos*," which means brothers and sisters.

"Worldwide, we're all firefighters no matter what," added 40-year-old Dan Regis of the Miramar Fire Department.

Some of the American firefighters were specifically trained to fight wildfires. They're called Hotshots and work in teams, known as handcrews, of about twenty men and women. Equipped with shovels, axes, chain saws, and sometimes a bulldozer, the Hotshots' job is to get in front of a wildfire and clear away trees and underbrush to create firebreaks.

Even with additional help, the San Diego County firefighters had to be selective about the fires they fought. In Poway, flames destroyed one hillside of homes while firefighters fought all night to save homes across the road. By morning, they were so exhausted they could barely talk, but they had won.

Some firefighters were especially heroic. Four of them, three men and a woman, attempted to rescue a father and his 15-year-old son who were trying to protect their home. The wind abruptly changed directions, and the fire trapped all six of them. A helicopter dropping water nearby managed to rescue

[NEXT PAGE] *Preparing to fight the fire.*
[© Nelvin C. Cepeda/U-T San Diego/ZUMAPress.com]

everyone except the father. Three of the four fire-fighters and the teenager were hospitalized, their condition critical. The boy had third-degree burns over half of his body. His father died in the fire.

The fast-paced fire worried San Diego Fire Rescue Battalion Chief John Tomson. "We're not going to stop it," he said. "I don't have any idea even where it is anymore. I'm not sure anybody knows where it is anymore." San Diego's 1.25 million residents weren't told to evacuate, but most businesses, government offices, and schools closed just in case.

One woman who decided to leave, Pat Helsing, compared the Witch Fire to the Cedar Fire four years earlier. The Cedar Fire had raced across the same region, burning 750,000 acres and 3,600 buildings and killing 24 people. "It seems scarier this time," she said. "The fire is everywhere. . . . You don't know where you can go to escape it."

Many people who were in the fire's path were trying to escape. MASSIVE EVACUATIONS ORDERED AS ONSLAUGHT OF FIRES SPREADS, proclaimed a front-page headline in the *Los Angeles Times*. It was the biggest evacuation in California's history. Nearly one-third of San Diego County's population, about 900,000 people, left their homes. Modern technology helped keep them informed.

Reverse 911, a computerized phone system, made

A firefighter silhouetted against the flames.
[© Ernie Grafton/U-T San Diego/ZUMAPress.com]

600,000 thirty-second calls, telling residents to evacuate. A newer system called Alert San Diego sent 400,000 phone, e-mail, and text messages over the Internet.

Residents Nate Ritter and Dan Tentler used Twitter and Flickr to make helpful posts. As often happens during natural disasters, people had rushed to

Heavy smoke hangs over north San Diego County. [U.S. Northern Command Public Affairs]

buy food and supplies, causing shortages. Tentler scouted supermarkets and convenience stores and then posted messages and photos of what was left on the shelves. Ritter's tweets combined bits of television and radio news with instant messages, e-mails, and text messages from evacuating people with helpful advice about traffic or lines at gas stations.

On Interstate 5, beneath a sky blackened by smoke, bumper-to-bumper cars and trucks inched northward toward Los Angeles. One reporter wrote that it looked like a scene from the movie *War of the Worlds*. Thousands of people slept in their cars beside highways, checked into motels, or moved to evacuation centers. The biggest evacuation center was Qualcomm Stadium, home of the San Diego Chargers, where officials prepared for 100,000 evacuees.

Many people left home with pets, both small and large. Some 1,500 evacuees along with 2,200 animals, including horses, chickens, and a zebra, found safety by the ocean at the Del Mar fairground and racetrack.

On Tuesday, two days after the Witch Fire began, the wind died down and firefighters extinguished the blaze just five miles from La Jolla and other oceanside communities. Officials then added up the losses. The fire destroyed 3,069 homes and other buildings and burned half a million acres, about one-fifth of the whole county. It killed 17 people. No firefighters died, but over one hundred were injured.

County residents heaped praised on the men and women who had fought the fires around the clock for three days. GOD BLESS OUR FIREFIGHTERS! said a sign in front of the Church at Rancho Bernardo. And a sign near the Bonita-Sunnyside fire station proclaimed FIRE FIGHTERS YOU ROCK.

Fire Chief Scott Walker said Bonita-Sunnyside residents had left thank-you notes and cupcakes at his station. "People have been very appreciative," Walker said, "but this is our job. We're proud to do it. It's called the fire service for that reason. We don't take that lightly."

From colonial bucket brigades to modern engines that can pump ten thousand gallons of water a minute, firefighting techniques and technology have evolved dramatically. But one thing hasn't changed over the centuries: the dedication and bravery of our firefighters.

People showed their appreciation for the firefighters in many ways. [© Sean DuFrene/U-T San Diego/ZUMAPress.com]

FIRE ENGINES IN AMERICAN HISTORY

1844. [LOC, USZ62-134241]

1852. [LOC, USZ62-134241]

1865. [LOC, USZ62-134241]

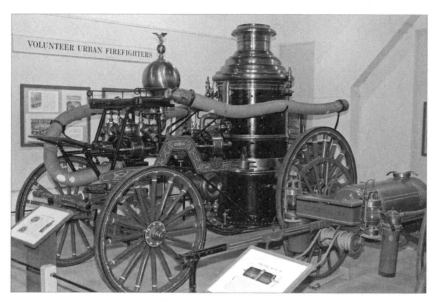

1878. [LOC, USZ62-134241]

1918. [LOC, USZ62-134241]

1919. [LOC, USZ62-134241]

1924. [LOC, USZ62-134241]

[BELOW] *1930.* [LOC, USZ62-134241]

1930. [LOC, USZ62-134241]

1937. [LOC, USZ62-134241]

1966. [LOC, USZ62-134241]

FIRE MUSEUMS TO VISIT

Many cities have fire museums where visitors can learn more about the history of firefighting.

Boston Fire Museum, 344 Congressional Street, Boston, MA 02210. Website: www.bostonfiremuseum.com.

Fire Museum of Greater Cincinnati, 115 West Court Street, Cincinnati, OH 45202.
Website: www.cincyfiremuseum.com.

Fire Museum of Maryland, 1301 York Road, Luthersville, MD 21093. Website: www.firemuseummd.org.

Fireman's Hall Museum, 147 North 2nd Street, Philadelphia, PA 19106. Website: www.firemanshall.org.

Hall of Flame, 6101 East Van Buren Street, Phoenix, AZ 85008. Website: www.hallofflame.org.

New York City Fire Museum, 278 Spring Street, New York, NY 10013. Website: www.nycfiremuseum.org.

San Francisco Fire Department Museum, 655 Presidio Avenue, San Francisco, CA 94115.
Website: www.guardiansofthecity.org.

RECOMMENDED READING

Brown, Don. *America Is Under Attack: The Day the Towers Fell.* New York: Roaring Brook Press, 2011.

Dwyer, Jim, and Kevin Flynn. *102 Minutes: The Untold Story of the Fight to Survive Inside the Twin Towers.* New York: Times Books, 2005.

Haddix, Margaret Peterson. *Uprising.* New York: Simon & Schuster, 2011.

Lee, Nancy, et al. *A Nation Challenged: A Visual History of 9/11 and Its Aftermath.* New York: Scholastic, 2002.

Marrin, Albert. *Flesh and Blood So Cheap: The Triangle Fire and Its Legacy.* New York: Knopf, 2011.

Murphy, Jim. *The Great Fire.* New York: Scholastic, 2006.

Nobleman, Marc Tyler. *The San Francisco Earthquake of 1906.* North Mankato, MN: Capstone, 2007.

O'Donnell, Edward T. *Ship Ablaze: The Tragedy of the Steamboat General Slocum.* New York: Broadway Books, 2003.

Tarshis, Lauren. *I Survived #5: I Survived the San Francisco Earthquake, 1906.* New York: Scholastic, 2012.

———. *I Survived #6: I Survived the Attacks of September 11, 2001.* New York: Scholastic, 2012.

WEBSITES
TO VISIT

Chicago History Museum, The Great Chicago Fire:
www.greatchicagofire.org/great-chicago-fire

City University of New York, Great Fire of 1835:
www.virtualny.cuny.edu/FIRE/welcome.html

Cornell University School of Industrial and Labor Relations,
Remembering the 1911 Triangle Factory Fire:
www.ilr.cornell.edu/trianglefire

Encyclopedia Titanica, The General Slocum: The Horror of
Fire at Sea:
www.encyclopedia-titanica.org/general-slocum.html

Maryland Digital Cultural Heritage Project, Great Baltimore
Fire of 1904:
www.mdch.org/fire/

Mass Moments, Boston Burns, March 20, 1760:
www.massmoments.com

Virtual Museum of the City of San Francisco, The Great
1906 Earthquake and Fire:
www.sfmuseum.org/1906/06.html

SOURCE NOTES

A note about citations: In most cases, quotations have not been altered and appear as originally written or published. In a few instances, punctuation or capitalization was adjusted to accommodate the incorporation of the quotation into the text.

Introduction

3 "dreadful city of fire": Brett Howard, *Boston: A Social History* (New York: Hawthorn Books, 1976), p. 289.

1. Colonial America's Biggest Fire: Boston, 1760

8 "noe man shall build his chimney": Dennis Smith, *History of Firefighting in America: 300 Years of Courage* (New York: Dial Press, 1976), p. 3.

8 "no dwelling house in Boston": ibid., p. 8.

10 "each Member": www.bostonfirehistory.org (accessed June 26, 2012).

11 "Brave men": Benjamin L. Carp, "Fire of Liberty," *The William and Mary Quarterly* 58 (2001): 785; available at http://www.jstor.org (accessed June 26, 2012).

11 "It is of some Importance": ibid., p. 786.

15 "While we were here the town": http://www.mass moments.org/index.cfm?mid=86 (accessed June 26, 2012).

15 "a perfect torrent of flame": Peter Charles Hoffer, *Seven*

Fires: The Urban Infernos That Reshaped America (New York: Public Affairs, 2006), p. 39.

16 "In the midst of our Distress": Donald J. Cannon, ed., *Heritage of Flames: The Illustrated History of Early American Firefighting* (New York: Doubleday, 1977), p. 129.

18 "Sermon Occasioned by the Great Fire": http://www .wallbuilders.com (accessed June 28, 2012).

20 "most humbly": Cannon, *Heritage of Flames*, p. 130.

2. A Terrible Torrent of Fire: New York, 1835

23 "How shall I record": Dennis Smith, *History of Firefighting in America: 300 Years of Courage* (New York: Dial Press, 1976), p. 41.

23 "The night was bitterly cold": William Callender, *Our Firemen, the History of the NY Fire Department*, http://www .newyorkroots.org/bookarchive/historyofnyfire departments/11-20/ch19pt6.html (accessed June 28, 2012).

24 "We managed to force open the door": Paul C. Ditzel, *Fire Engines, Firefighters: The Men, Equipment, and Machines, from Colonial Days to the Present* (New York: Crown, 1976), p. 83.

28 "with glowing redness": ibid., p. 85.

31 "I stood at the corner": Callender, *Our Firemen*.

31 "Street after street": A. E. Costello, *Our Firemen: The History of the New York Fire Department from 1609 to 1887* (New York: Tom Doherty Associates, 2002), p. 254.

32 "The water looked": ibid., p. 288.

32 "The heart of the city": ibid., p. 289.

33 The one-billion-dollar estimate is from Measuringworth .com (accessed June 5, 2013).

3. America's Most Famous Fire: Chicago, 1871

38 "the Gem of the Prairie": Jim Murphy, *The Great Fire* (New York: Scholastic, 1995), p. 46.

43 "The wind had increased to a tempest": ibid., p. 43.

44 "CHICAGO IS IN FLAMES": ibid., p. 46.

45 "Suddenly there came a crash": greatchicagofire.org (accessed June 26, 2012).

45 "The scene was now": ibid.

47 "a torrent of humanity": Murphy, *The Great Fire*, p. 62.

47 "was utterly choked": greatchicagofire.org.

51 "In some instances": ibid.

52 "Heaps of ruins": Murphy, *The Great Fire*, p. 89.

52 The $4 billion estimate is from Measuringworth.com (accessed June 5, 2013).

4. New Century, Old Problem: Baltimore, 1904

58 "nurseries where the youth": Dennis Smith, *History of Firefighting in America: 300 Years of Courage* (New York: Dial Press, 1976), p. 59.

63 "We're in God's Hands": Peter Charles Hoffer, *Seven Fires: The Urban Infernos That Reshaped America* (New York: Public Affairs, 2006), p. 171.

63 "Throughout the terrible contest": "Flames Raged for Nearly 40 Hours," *New York Times*, February 9, 1904.

64 "sent their fierce tongues": "$400,000 Loss in Baltimore; Business Section of the City Swept Away by Flames Which Raged All of Sunday," *New York Times*, February 8, 1904.

65 "Great multitudes of people": ibid.

65 "we knew then": Marion Elizabeth Rogers, *Mencken: The*

American Iconoclast (New York: Oxford University Press, 2005), p. 81.

65 "the great army of firefighters": "Baltimore Saved, Loss $150,000,000: Fire Controlled, but City Stunned by Its Greatest Disaster," *New York Times*, February 9, 1904.

67 "During all of these hours": "Progress of the Flames," *New York Times,* February 8, 1904.

68 "a flock of great white fowl": "Flames Raged for Nearly 40 Hours."

69 "Again and again": ibid.

69 "Where at Saturday's close of business": "Baltimore Saved."

72 "to say that the structure": Hoffer, *Seven Fires,* p. 183.

73 only 18 of the 48 largest U.S. cities: http://www.fire.nist .gov/bfrlpubs/fire04/PDF/f04095.pdf (accessed June 26, 2012).

5. Fire on the Water: New York, 1904

75 "There was never a happier party": Jim Kalafus, "The General Slocum: The Horror of Fire at Sea," http://www .encyclopedia-titanica.org/general-slocum.html (accessed June 26, 2012).

79 "Get the hell out of here": *Newsday*, April 10, 2009.

80 "I saw smoke": Kalafus, "The General Slocum."

81 "there was a roar": Edward T. O'Donnell, *Ship Ablaze: The Tragedy of the Steamboat General Slocum* (New York: Broadway Books, 2003), p. 111.

84 "the flames burst": Kalafus, "The General Slocum."

84 "the fire drove me back": O'Donnell, *Ship Ablaze*, p. 107.

84 "thought that the boat": Kalafus, "The General Slocum."

85 "Sheets of flame": ibid.

85 "Thinking the little girl": ibid.

86 "Unclasping my knife": ibid.

86 "My wife and I stood": ibid.

86 "Twenty would jump": ibid.

89 "After papa tied": ibid.

90 "I went overboard": ibid.

90 "I didn't have no life preserver": ibid.

90 "To my dying day": ibid.

6. America's Last Great Urban Fire: San Francisco, 1906

95 Crown Jewel of the Pacific: http://www.sfmuseum.org (accessed June 27, 2012).

97 "At No. 313 Sixth St.": "Operations of the San Francisco Fire Department Following 1906 Great Earthquake and Fire of April 18, 1906," http://www.sfmuseum.org /conflag/06index.html (accessed June 26, 2012).

99 "swirling up the narrow way": Carl Nolte, "The Great Quake: 1906–2006/The Great Fire," *San Francisco Chronicle*, April 12, 2006.

102 "the lower portion of Market Street": http://www. sfmuseum.org/conflag/06index.html (accessed June 26, 2012).

105 "there being considerable water": "Experience of Captain Charles J. Cullen Engine No. 6 and His Men," http://www.sfmuseum.org/conflag/e6.html (accessed July 1, 2012).

105 "We laid a line": "Experience of Battalion Chief John McClusky," http://www.sfmuseum.org/conflag/batt1 .html (accessed July 1, 2012).

105 "Many of them dropped": "The Dire Calamity and the Greater San Francisco," http://www.sfmuseum.org /1906.2/dire.html (accessed July 1, 2012).

106 "When opportunity afforded": "George F. Brown Captain, San Francisco Fire Department Engine Company 2," http://www.sfmuseum.org/conflag/e2 .html (accessed June 26, 2012).

106 "thousands of families": "Account of Louise Herrick Wall," http://www.sfmuseum.org/1906.2/ew24.html (accessed July 1, 2012).

106 "It was an earth-racked": Nolte, "The Great Quake."

107 "The great stand": "Jack London and the Great Earthquake and Fire," http://www.sfmuseum.org/hist5 /jlondon.html (accessed June 28, 2012).

109 "Not in history": ibid.

7. Deadly Workplace Fire: New York, 1911

116 "Fire. There is a fire, Mr. Bernstein": David Von Drehle, *Triangle: The Fire That Changed America* (New York: Grove Press, 2003), p. 228.

117 "Get out of here as fast as you can": ibid., p. 238.

118 "I ran to the Washington Place door": "Girls Fought Vainly at Triangle Doors," *New York Times*, December 12, 1911.

119 "all I could see": Von Drehle, *Triangle,* p. 289.

119 "I reached out": "Stories of Survivors and Witnesses and Rescuers Outside Tell What They Saw," *New York Times,* March 26, 1911.

121 "Horrified and helpless": Louis Waldman, *Labor Lawyer* (New York: E. P. Dutton, 1944), p. 32.

8. Nightclub Tragedy: Boston, 1942

129 "It was so crowded": Casey C. Grant, "Last Dance at the Cocoanut Grove," *NFPA Journal*, November/December 2007, http://www.nfpa.org/publicJournalDetail.asp?categoryID=1517&itemID=36513&cookie_test=1 (accessed July 1, 2012).

131 "There was a flash": Boyd Magers, "Cocoanut Grove Controversy," *Western Clippings*, #8, November/December 1995.

131 "The closer I was": Grant, "Last Dance at the Cocoanut Grove."

133 "We had just been served": David Wallechinsky and Irving Wallace, *The People's Almanac #2* (New York: Morrow, 1975).

134 "It was incredible": Grant, "Last Dance at the Cocoanut Grove."

137 "The tables weren't all burnt": ibid.

137 "Of all the vivid impressions": ibid.

140 "At the time": ibid.

9. 9/11: Fire in the Sky: New York, 2001

152 "large volume of fire": *The 9/11 Commission Report: Final Report of the National Commission on Terrorist Attacks upon the United States* (Washington, D.C.: 2004), p. 291.

152 "We had a very strong sense": ibid., p. 290.

154 "I'm SCARED": Jim Dwyer and Kevin Flynn, *102 Minutes: The Untold Story of the Fight to Survive Inside the Twin Towers* (New York: Times Books, 2004), p. 41.

155 "Where are you guys going?": ibid., p. 64.

156 "dodging bodies": Richard Picciotto and Daniel Paisner,

Last Man Down: A Firefighter's Story of Survival and Escape from the World Trade Center (New York: Berkley Books, 2002), p. 36.

158 "All units, tower 1": Peter Charles Hoffer, *Seven Fires: The Urban Infernos That Reshaped America* (New York: Public Affairs, 2006), p. 337.

159 "a bone-chilling roar": Picciotto and Paisner, *Last Man Down*, p. 65.

159 "Get out!": ibid., p. 69.

162 "And as they moved toward me": ibid., p. 92.

162 "earsplitting, bone-chilling": ibid., p. 101.

162 "Whatever it was": ibid., p. 111.

165 A total of 412 rescue workers died: Dwyer and Flynn, *102 Minutes*, p. xxiv.

10. Wildfire: San Diego County, 2007

173 "was fast, hard, furious": Scott Gold and Ari B. Bloomekatz, "Tasting Soot and Defeat," *Los Angeles Times*, October 25, 2007.

175 "The perimeter of the fire is huge": Garrett Therolf and James Ricci, "This was hardly a fair fight," *Los Angeles Times*, October 24, 2007.

176 "There isn't a difference": from Ari B. Bloomekatz, "Mexican Fire Crew Joins the Fight," *Los Angeles Times*, October 27, 2007.

177 "Worldwide, we're all firefighters": Bloomekatz, "Mexican Fire Crew."

180 "We're not going to stop it": Tony Perry et al., "Massive Evacuations Ordered as Onslaught of Fires Spreads," *Los Angeles Times*, October 23, 2007.

180 "It seems scarier this time": ibid.

180 MASSIVE EVACUATIONS ORDERED: ibid.

183 One reporter wrote: ibid.

184 GOD BLESS OUR FIREFIGHTERS!: Janine Zúñiga, "Firefighters
See an Outpouring of Gratitude," *San Diego
Union-Tribune*, October 27, 2007.

184 "People have been very appreciative": ibid.

GLOSSARY

conflagration. A large fire.

engine company. A group of firefighters assigned to an apparatus equipped with water pump, fire hose, and other firefighting tools.

firebrands. Airborne embers.

firebreak. An open space cleared as much as possible of flammable material.

fire codes. Regulations that help prevent fires.

fire drill. A practiced method of getting people out of buildings during emergencies in a calm and orderly way.

fire inspector. Someone who issues permits, inspects buildings, and enforces fire codes.

firestorm. Strong currents of air drawn into a blaze, making it more intense.

flashover. When everything flammable in a room or small building catches fire all at once.

Halligan bar. A firefighter's tool that's like a combination of an ax and a pick, used for forcing open doors.

overhauling. Looking for coals or embers that could rekindle a fire.

pumper. A fire truck equipped with a pump and a water tank.

rollover. Ignition of ceiling-level fire gases.

turn out. Respond to a fire.

turnout gear. Protective clothing worn by firefighters.

BIBLIOGRAPHY

Books

Burgess-Wise, David. *Fire Engines & Fire-Fighting*. London: Octopus Books, 1977.

Burrows, Edwin G., et al. *Gotham: A History of New York City to 1898*. New York: Oxford University Press, 1999.

Callender, William. *Our Firemen, the History of the NY Fire Department*. See http://www.newyorkroots.org /bookarchive/historyofnyfiredepartments/11-20.

Cannon, Donald J., ed. *Heritage of Flames: The Illustrated History of Early American Firefighting*. New York: Doubleday, 1977.

Costello, A. E. *Birth of the Bravest*. New York: Tom Doherty Associates, 2002. Google eBook.

———. *Our Firemen: The History of the New York Fire Department from 1609 to 1887*. New York: Tom Doherty Associates, 2002.

Ditzel, Paul C. *Fire Engines, Firefighters: The Men, Equipment, and Machines, from Colonial Days to the Present*. New York: Crown, 1976.

Dwyer, Jim, and Kevin Flynn. *102 Minutes: The Untold Story of the Fight to Survive Inside the Twin Towers*. New York: Times Books, 2005.

Glanz, James, and Eric Lipton. *City in the Sky: The Rise and Fall of the World Trade Center*. New York: Times Books, 2003.

Hoffer, Peter Charles. *Seven Fires: The Urban Infernos That Reshaped America*. New York: Public Affairs, 2006.

Hone, Philip. *The Diary of Philip Hone, 1828–1851*. New York: Dodd, Mead, 1889. Google eBook.

Howard, Brett. *Boston: A Social History*. New York: Hawthorn Books, 1976.

Keyes, Edward. *Cocoanut Grove*. New York: Atheneum, 1984.

King, William T. *History of the American Steam Fire-Engine*. Mineola, NY: Dover Publications, 2001.

Loeper, John L. *By Hook & Ladder*. New York: Atheneum, 1981.

Murphy, Jim. *The Great Fire*. New York: Scholastic, 1995.

O'Donnell, Edward T. *Ship Ablaze: The Tragedy of the Steamboat General Slocum*. New York: Broadway Books, 2003.

Picciotto, Richard, and Daniel Paisner. *Last Man Down: A Firefighter's Story of Survival and Escape from the World Trade Center*. New York: Berkley Books, 2002.

Rogers, Marion Elizabeth. *Mencken: The American Iconoclast*. New York: Oxford University Press, 2005.

Smith, Dennis. *History of Firefighting in America: 300 Years of Courage*. New York: Dial Press, 1976.

———. *Firefighters*. New York: Doubleday, 1988.

Von Drehle, David. *Triangle: The Fire That Changed America*. New York: Grove Press, 2003.

Waldman, Louis. *Labor Lawyer*. New York: E. P. Dutton, 1944.

Warden, G. B. *Boston 1689–1776*. Boston: Little, Brown, 1970.

Winchester, Simon. *A Crack in the Edge of the World: America and the Great California Earthquake of 1906*. New York: HarperCollins, 2005.

Newspapers and Journals

Bloomekatz, Ari B. "Mexican Fire Crew Joins the Fight." *Los Angeles Times*, October 27, 2007.

Carp, Benjamin L. "Fire of Liberty: Firefighters, Urban Voluntary Culture and the Revolutionary Movement." *The William and Mary Quarterly*, 58 (2001).

Gold, Scott, and Ari B. Bloomekatz. "Tasting Soot and Defeat." *Los Angeles Times*, October 25, 2007.

Grant, Casey C. "Last Dance at the Cocoanut Grove." *NFPA Journal,* November/December 2007.

Magers, Boyd. "Cocoanut Grove Controversy," *Western Clippings*, No. 8, November-December 1995.

New York Times. "Baltimore Saved, Loss $150,000,000; Fire Controlled, but City Stunned by Its Greatest Disaster," February 9, 1904.

———. "$400,000 Loss in Baltimore; Business Section of the City Swept Away by Flames Which Raged All of Sunday," February 8, 1904.

———. "Stories of Survivors and Witnesses and Rescuers Outside Tell What They Saw," March 26, 1911.

———. "Girls Fought Vainly at Triangle Doors," December 12, 1911.

Nolte, Carl. "The Great Quake: 1906–2006/The Great Fire." *San Francisco Chronicle,* April 12, 2006.

Perry, Tony, et al. "Massive Evacuations Ordered as Onslaught of Fires Spreads." *Los Angeles Times*, October 23, 2007.

Zúñiga, Janine. "Firefighters See an Outpouring of Gratitude." *San Diego Union-Tribune*, October 27, 2007.

Internet

Boston Fire Historical Society. "Boston History Before 1859." See www.bostonfirehistory.org/historybostonbefore1859.html.

Chicago Historical Society and the Trustees of Northwestern University. "The Great Chicago Fire and the Web of Memory." See www.greatchicagofire.org.

City of Chicago. "History of the Chicago Fire Department." June 10, 1904. See www.chicagofd.org/historyofthecfd .html.

City University of New York. "Great Fire of December 1835." See www.virtualny.cuny.edu/FIRE/welcome.html.

Cornell University School of Industrial and Labor Relations. "The Triangle Factory Fire." See www.ilr.cornell.edu /trianglefire/.

Kalafus, Jim. "The General Slocum: The Horror of Fire at Sea." See www.encyclopedia-titanica.org/general-slocum .html.

Maryland Digital Cultural Heritage. "The Great Baltimore Fire of 1904." See www.mdch.org/fire/#.

Massachusetts Foundation for the Humanities. "Boston Burns. March 20, 1760." See www.massmoments.org.

Mayhew, Jonathan. "A Sermon Occasioned by the Great Fire in Boston, New-England." See www.wallbuilders.com.

Seck, Momar D., and David D. Evans. "Major U.S. Cities Using National Standard Fire Hydrants One Century After the Great Baltimore Fire." See www.fire.nist.gov.

Trivia Library. "Natural Disasters: The Cocoanut Grove Fire in Boston in 1942, History and Account of the Tragedy, Death, and Destruction." See www.Trivia-Library.com.

Virtual Museum of the City of San Francisco. "Account of Louise Herrick Wall." See www.sfmuseum.org/1906.2 /ew24.html.

———. "The Dire Calamity and the Greater San Francisco Earthquake and Fire." See www.sfmuseum.org/1906.2 /dire.html.

———. "Experience of Battalion Chief John McClusky." See www.sfmuseum.org/conflag/batt1.html.

———. "George F. Brown Captain, San Francisco Fire Department Engine Company 2." See www.sfmuseum.org /conflag/e2.html.

———. "Jack London and the Great Earthquake and Fire." See www.sfmuseum.org/hist5/jlondon.html.

INDEX

Page numbers in *italics* refer to illustrations.